The Causes Of Sales Success

The Key to Navigating The Maze of Sales

Tom Payne

The Causes of Sales Success

The Key to Navigating
The Maze of Sales

Copyright © 2012 by Tom Payne

ISBN-13: 978-1480224636

ISBN-10: 1480224634

All rights reserved. No part of this book may be used or reproduced by any means, graphic, electronic, or mechanical, including photocopying, recording, taping, or by any information storage retrieval system without the written permission of the author except in the case of brief quotations embodied in critical articles and reviews.

Published by EGS Publishing

An imprint of Essential Growth Solutions, LLC

Chicago, IL

To salespeople—

Companies depend on your success.

Contents

Acknowledgments	ix
Preface	x

Part One: Navigating the Maze of Sales   1

1. The Key to the Maze	3
2. The Power of Perception	15
3. Power Questions	28
4. Consultative Selling	42
5. To Be First Is…	53

Part Two: Powerful Presentations   63

6. Differentiation Is Powerful	65
7. Powerful Stories	78
8. The Power of Words	89
9. Presentation Power	97

Part Three: Finishing Touches   107

10. The Mindset of a Champion	109
11. Relationships	118
12. After the Sale	129
13. Sales Performance Coaching	136

Part Four: Everyone Sells — 151

14. Interviewing — 153
15. Fulfillment — 165

Acknowledgements

Special thanks go to Maureen Pajerski, who provided me with an environment of support that allowed creativity to flourish. She gave me the time, space and encouragement to develop the sales training concepts and workshops that make up the heart of this book.

I worked closely with our marketing department, headed by Larry Ball. He, and three of his team members—Jennifer Holden, Kelly Daly and Sandy Clavey—gave the training classes an added depth.

My sales managers confirmed these skills were transferrable. There are many deserving mention, but I will limit it to two: Sean Doherty and Kevin Hickey, two leaders of my Irish mafia. (As we grew it seemed like the only interview candidates I ever saw were Irish in their ethnicity, and they were good, so I hired them.)

One book on sales, above all others, made a strong impression on me at an early stage of my career. *Managing Major Sales*, by Neil Rackham and Richard Ruff, showed me how there were simple sales (typically involving one decision maker and a small amount of money), and complex sales (multiple decision makers and larger price tags), and the two categories operated in very different ways. It also gave me valuable instruction on how to coach a salesperson effectively.

Finally, I am always grateful to my wife, Joni, for her love, support and editorial guidance. As a sales star in her own right, she taught me about the power of strong relationships with customers and how they can lead to enduring friendships long after the sales relationship ends.

Preface

We were growing at our competitor's expense and were starting to recruit their most talented salespeople. While I was interviewing one of them I asked, "Why are you interested in leaving [our competitor] and joining us?"

Her answer was telling: "I want to find out what kind of magic pixie dust you are sprinkling on your sales managers that keeps me from winning any sales lately."

We should not have been winning so many sales. We were smaller than most of our competitors, including the one she worked for, by a large margin. Two of these competitors generated over $30 billion in revenue, and another was over $2 billion dollars in size. Meanwhile, our division was under $100 million in revenue even after doubling in size. I mention this detail because size matters when you are selling systems to hospitals that can cost upwards of $3 million dollars installed. They don't want to invest that amount of money on a company that a) might not be around, and b) they've never heard of.

"Magic pixie dust." I smiled and thought, "Her answer shows how our competitors are lost in the maze of sales and they don't know how to find their way out. What we are doing is not magic. If we hire her I will tell her how we sell, and she will think, 'This is nothing but common sense.'"

I then responded to her "pixie dust" comment, "Once you are part of the team you will see that it is not magic, but sometimes it sure seems like it."

Part One:

Navigating the Maze of Sales

1: The Key to the Maze

For Every Effect, There Is a Cause

What causes a customer to make a buying decision? Or, to ask this question in the language of sales, what causes a sale to close? The answer to this question is critical. For if we don't know what *causes* a sale, then how can we cause one? Until we *know* how to cause the buying-decision-effect, our selling is guesswork. We are like people trying to navigate a difficult maze while blindfolded.

A profession must know what causes the outcome it desires, or it is condemned to wander lost. For example, European physicians once believed they caused healing by correcting fluid imbalances in the body. Since blood was the body's primary fluid, they would surgically open a patient's vein and let them bleed to correct some of these imbalances. Bleeding was practiced for over 2000 years (!) until medical professionals began to understand what caused the effect of healing and health.[1]

---

[1] Hippocrates was born around 460 BC and died around 370 BC. He was the father of western medicine and he believed in the theory of health being controlled by the four fluids of the body. This view was still being held, and practiced, by some physicians in the nineteenth century. For example Lord Byron, the famous English poet, was bled to treat an illness in 1824. His death, several days later, may have been caused by this "therapy."

The Causes of Sales Success

Before anyone in the sales profession judges these pioneer-physicians too harshly, we should first make certain that we are not repeating their mistake. Do salespeople know what causes the outcome they desire, namely, the closed sale?

First, let's examine what salespeople do in their attempt to close a sale. They present features and benefits, ask probing questions, sell in a consultative fashion, develop strong relationships and ask for the order: Close, close, close. This causes the closed sale, right? No. These techniques fail to account for the following:

> I have walked into situations where our company was loathed (they loved the competitor), our sales manager was tossed out of the account, the first five minutes of my presentation were dominated by the customer hurling abuse at my company, our product and me. Yet, after one hour, the tables were turned and I closed the sale.

How? It wasn't by presenting features and benefits; the customer would have yawned at me while I tried to walk down this well-trodden road. Since I was called in from the corporate office to present at the last minute there was no time to ask probing questions, or perform the analysis typically used in the consultative sales process, so consultative selling could not have been a cause of this closed sale. It certainly wasn't closed through the strength of my relationships as the decision-making group made quite clear. Finally, I never asked for their order. Not once, much less three times. However, their unlikely buying decision came about because I knowingly employed the causes that produce the buying-decision-effect.

So, what are these causes? Our quest to find this answer begins by answering the simple question: "What is selling?"

It is the art of causing a buying decision.

This simple definition tells us that selling is subject to the peculiarities of human psychology, because *decisions are made by the mind*. The question now becomes, "What are the psychological causes of the buying-decision?"

Let's consider the broadest categories of influence: Is the decision rational or emotional? Are people sold by logical arguments or by emotional ones? It depends on what you are selling.

Simple Sales

If someone sells a product that is relatively inexpensive, then the buying decision has little risk. Since the buyer doesn't fear the consequences of his decision, there is little emotion involved in making one. Also, one person makes this decision. There is no need to convene a meeting, or form a committee, to decide on buying something when it has little impact on the organization.

The rule for selling in this situation is: *Close, close, close.* After all, the one who can make the decision is standing right in front of you, and if he is nudged toward a decision by your closing attempts, then perhaps he will decide in your favor.

Complex Sales

Complex sales are different. They typically involve more than one decision maker and the dollar amounts for goods and services can go from thousands to millions of dollars. If you were to offer your complex sales product to a decision-making team, and then try to close them, they would likely laugh. Their buying decision comes at the end of a multi-step process. Until this process is completed, your closing attempts will be ignored.

In complex sales—the subject of this book—*the causes of the buying decision are emotional in nature.*

Before going further let's make sure this assumption is true, because if it is, then our entire approach to sales needs to be modified and, in some cases, completely overhauled.

Emotional Decisions and Money

The sales system detailed in this book was taught to many sales classes over the course of a week, and I would typically begin them with a question: "Is the buying decision for our product rational or emotional?"

The Causes of Sales Success

The majority would always answer: *Rational*. Since our product could cost millions installed, they assumed it would have to be as rational as possible. They naturally thought, "No one would allow their emotions to dictate how they would invest many thousands or even millions of dollars."

Then I would ask, "As we increase the dollar amount of the purchase does the decision become more rational or less rational?" This usually made them think a little bit longer. Some would begin to connect the dots and answer, "Less rational."

The buying decision in complex sales is emotional and becomes more so as the dollar amount of the sale goes up. The more money, the more emotion, because money is emotion quantified.

IBM, with its very expensive computer systems, helps prove this point. During its time of total market dominance a saying developed: "Nobody ever got fired for buying IBM."

Where is the logic in that? Here we have a seemingly rational buyer, an engineer or Information Technology (IT) professional, being swayed by the emotion of fear. In other words, the fear of being responsible for making a bad decision on such an expensive and important system caused people to decide for the tried and true IBM system. From this we can see how the engineer is as vulnerable as the poet to the tidal sweep of emotion.

Economists understand the causal relationship between emotions and buying decisions. One of their most important gauges is the Consumer *Sentiment* Index. It measures how the consumer *feels* about the current economy, their own prospects and the future of the economy. If they are fearful of their own prospects, and the economic future of the country, then how likely is it that they will spend the same amount as they did during times when they were *feeling* optimistic and carefree?

Fears of one's future prospects, and the outlook of the economy, produce cautious buying behavior and are predictive of slowdowns in consumer spending. Economists have not thought it necessary to create a Consumer Rationality Index, because making buying decisions—spending significant sums of money—is governed more by emotions than by reason.

An Example Closer to Home

Finally, consider the husband and wife who are in the market for a home. They agree upon a budget of $250,000. This is the upper limit of what they are willing to pay. They can afford more, but they do not want to be house-poor for the next five-to-ten years. This is very rational.

Unfortunately for these rational homebuyers, they have an "irrational" realtor. What does she do? She takes them into five to ten homes in the specified range, and then into a house that goes for $275,000. Why is she wasting her time and theirs?

The couple enters the house with their guard up: "Didn't we tell her $250,000 was the limit?" Then they see what a bigger mortgage translates into and their thoughts become, "This home is so much nicer. Look at the closet space and the nicer appliances. The realtor said the price is not a problem. I love this place. Wouldn't we just love living here?"

What just happened? Two very rational people confronting what might be the largest purchasing decision of their lives started the home-buying process with rational rules in place. But once they walked into a "much" nicer home, their emotional response to the prospect of living there chucked their rational rules out the window.

Should we accept this assumption—emotions cause the buying decision in complex sales—and move on? No, not yet. For if we start with the wrong assumption, then we are doomed to draw wrong conclusions, like the physicians who assumed health was regulated by the balance of fluids in the body. Is there a way to test this assumption before embracing it? Yes.

Verifying the Cause

Since philosophers have been studying the subject of causality for thousands of years, let's take advantage of their intense noodling. I will quote a sentence from the philosopher David Hume, and then

The Causes of Sales Success

paraphrase it to make it both easier to understand and relevant to our search for the cause of closed sales.

Hume wrote:

> ...where several different objects produce the same effect, it must be by means of some quality, which we discover to be common amongst them.[2]

Which can be paraphrased as follows: "Where several different [sales systems and techniques] produce the same effect [the buying decision], it must be by means of some quality [emotion?], which we discover to be common amongst them." In other words, if we look at the most effective techniques and sales systems, they should share an emotional approach to selling. So let's see if this holds true.

Most selling systems emphasize the importance of relationships because of the undeniable influence they exert on a buying decision. Are not relationships based on emotions? Yes, but as will be shown, we will need to refine our understanding of relationships if we are to turn them into a cause of the buying decision.

What about the technique of finding out what a customer's "hot button" is? Most selling systems also emphasize the importance of this. If there was ever an emotion-based approach it is this one. Reason is cool and dispassionate; it has no hot button. A customer's excitement about the solution a product provides is an emotional response and not a rational one.

Other systems promote a consultative selling style, and this can be quite effective. On its surface consultative selling seems to be a completely rational approach devoid of emotion. But consider what the consultant is hoping to uncover with his questions and research. Is he not trying to discover what frustrates the customer and makes them want to scream? This is typically one of his goals, because if the consultative salesperson can solve those problems that are the most vexing, then he will give the buyer a strong incentive to decide for his offering.

---

[2] David Hume, *A Treatise of Human Nature* (Digireads.com Publishing, 2010), p. 104.

The Key to the Maze

If you are in sales, you've probably experienced this. You present a solution that will get rid of a truly annoying problem and someone in the audience cannot contain their excitement. They blurt out things like, "Sold!" and, "We've got to have that!" The consultative sales approach is a method of uncovering hot buttons. It maps out the customer's emotional landscape.

Let's return to Hume's insight on causation and paraphrase it: "Where several different sales systems and techniques produce buying decisions, it is by means of the quality of emotion, which we discover to be common amongst them." In looking at some of the most-admired approaches to selling, we see the common element of their emotional orientation.

Consultative Selling Transformed

Here is the problem with the consultative approach, or any other that is not based on what causes the buying decision. If you do not know that emotions cause the buying decision, you may uncover vital information through consultative techniques and fail to use it as effectively as possible. In other words, you may treat every uncovered need the same, and give less weight to the truly emotional drivers of the buying decision.

Worse still, the consultant who does not know what causes the closed sale may look for what irritates the customer, but fail to look for what makes them fearful, or what hopes and dreams they are trying to satisfy with this purchase. If his competitor knows this information and shows how his product satisfies the customer's emotional needs, and closes the sale, then was this closed sale the result of his consultative approach?

No, because both individuals were using consultative selling styles. What closed the sale was the uncovering of powerful emotions and presenting in a way that tapped into them. The competitor showed how the customer's hopes could be met by his product, why they should fear using any other product, and these emotions and others caused their decision: sold!

Relationships Transformed

The same is true about one's view of relationships. Sales are not closed by relationships but by the emotions they generate.

This may sound too nuanced, but it is not. The difference is very important. For example, if I believe relationships close sales, then, whenever I visit my customers, I might choose to be the much-loved life of the party. I am entertaining, and customers love to have me around every so often to liven up their day. As a result, I have good relationships throughout my territory.

However, I've met salespeople with great personalities who had good relationships across their territory and they were middle-of-the-pack performers. If relationships cause buying decisions, then why weren't they top performers?

Now let's look at the salesperson who has relationships that generate an emotion that causes sales to close in her favor. She is liked, but also *trusted*. Trust is a very powerful emotion. It is important to be liked, and it is good to be entertaining, but it is better to be trusted. Trust will win the sale because it quiets a customer's fears over making a bad decision that might haunt them for years. IBM was a trusted company, with trusted representatives, and nobody ever got fired for buying IBM.[3]

In the above example both salespeople have excellent relationships with their customers, but one is liked and does an average job, and the other is both liked and trusted and excels. Therefore, it is not the relationship that closes the sale, but the emotions the relationship generates.

---

[3] English is a wonderful language, but when it comes to gender it falls short. For example, there is no gender-neutral pronoun that means both she and he, or her and his. Previously, all references found in books were uniformly masculine. Lately I've seen books use exclusively feminine pronouns. This seems to be a mistake made in the other direction. For this reason I will sometimes use masculine and sometimes use feminine references, and ask for forgiveness if I seem to favor one gender over the other.

This subtle difference in the way we look at relationships leads to important changes in what we do and how we sell. Instead of trying to develop a relationship with a customer, we try to develop a bond of trust, and there are specific things we can do to accomplish this.

Here is the point. Until we understand how the decision is emotionally driven, will we ever systematically approach consultative selling or the development of relationships in this way? No. But once we understand how emotions cause closed sales we will start to look at the consultative approach, the building of relationships, and everything else in a new light. We will modify existing techniques and create new ones so that we may cause our sales success.

What the Rest of the Book Will Cover

The unlit, confusing maze of sales is human nature. All salespeople must navigate this course. When we run into its walls we find they are immovable and unforgiving. We cannot go through them, or scale over them; we are simply required to follow them, because we cannot change human nature. This book is an attempt to provide a key to understanding this dark maze from a sales perspective. What follows are the subjects we will cover to accomplish this task.

Part One: Navigating the Maze of Sales

The remaining chapters of *Part One* are aimed at deepening our understanding of the sales process, and preparing salespeople to deliver presentations that irresistibly lead the customer to choose their product or service.

Since emotions cause closed sales, how do we generate powerful and positive emotions? In the next chapter, *The Power of Perception*, we will look at how perceptions generate emotions, and the ways salespeople can change how they, and their product, are perceived. Much of the rest of the book is based on the insights contained in this chapter.

How do we develop questions that unearth emotionally powerful information? The chapter entitled, *Power Questions,* shows how. Not all questions work. Some produce information that is inconsequential and potentially misleading. We need a simple process to develop questions custom-tailored to each unique decision maker and decision influencer.

This process of developing effective questions was the basis of a popular workshop, and this brings up an important point. All of the ideas in this book were refined in dozens of classrooms and thoroughly field-tested in intense selling situations, several of which will be used as illustrations. In other words, this book is not based on theoretical musings—don't let my quoting a philosopher fool you—but on hard-fought sales contests that mostly ended in victory. Those that didn't result in wins revealed important emotional reasons why we failed, and they will be covered.

In *Consultative Sales,* we redesign the consultative approach so that it helps the customer make the emotional migration from fear to trust, and then partnership.

In the chapter *To Be First Is…* we look at the tremendous advantage a salesperson gains by finding an opportunity before anyone else. It also shows how you can find these opportunities first, and why you always want to be the first salesperson to present. One of the primary reasons we lost sales was arriving late on the scene.

Part Two: Powerful Presentations

The chapter entitled, *Differentiation Is Powerful*, will introduce you to a technique that is contrary to what salespeople are typically taught. The seemingly impossible sales situation that I depicted above—where I was called in to present to a hostile crowd at the last minute—was turned around by differentiation. Some of the results generated by this technique still have me shaking my head in amazement.

The chapter on *Powerful Stories* will help you make your presentation memorable and entertaining. People do not remember statistics, and their minds retreat in the face of a data dump, but a good story engages the mind. This is critical in a complex sale, particularly after a customer has listened to five consecutive, one-hour-long presentations. If yours is the only one that held their attention, and used a format that is inherently memorable, then won't you possess a powerful advantage? This story-telling technique was the subject of another popular workshop in our training program.

Since words can create emotions powerful enough to move a nation to redress wrongs—the civil rights movement—then how can a salesperson harness the emotional power of words? *The Power of Words* shows how to develop memorable phrases that grow in power as they are repeated.

Part Two's last chapter, *Presentation Power,* looks at ways of changing the style of the presentation to engage and hold the customer's attention. In some cases, this presentation style and content resulted in customers requesting my presentation so they could use it internally to sell other members of the decision-making team. It is safe to say this improved our chances of closing the sale.

Part Three: Finishing Touches

We need to win the war within. Our attitudes can sometimes be the most self-defeating baggage that we choose to carry through life, and they affect our sales success as well. In *The Mindset of a Champion* we look at how some of the most important attitudes we can adopt are often ones we shy away from.

Relationships exert a powerful influence on sales decisions because of the emotions they generate. But how do we establish relationships that generate the most powerful and favorable emotions? The chapter entitled *Relationships* goes over a plan to develop them in a way that both causes sales success and the satisfaction that can come from strong and enduring friendships.

What do many salespeople do *After the Sale?* They move on to the next sales target and forget about the person who just gave them their business. This approach can cause a salesperson to lose *the most powerful sales tool of all*. Unlike differentiation, the salesperson is not doing the selling, the satisfied customer is.

Sales Performance Coaching is a chapter on how to drive the adoption of successful behaviors in each individual of a sales team. This chapter is ideally for sales managers, one of corporate America's most under-utilized assets. It provides them with a skill that enables them to have a greater impact on revenue growth than probably any other position in the company.

Salespeople should also read this chapter on coaching to see if they are benefiting from this practice. They probably aren't, because few corporations, large or small, train their sales managers in this much-needed skill. So, if your sales manager is not coaching you, then share with them the ideas in this chapter. After all, it is possible to coach the coach.

Part Four: Everyone Sells

If you have purchased this book and are not involved with sales or marketing, then I congratulate you for stepping outside of your comfort zone to learn a powerful, helpful new skill. Nowhere is this need to be able to sell more obvious, or critical to one's financial well being, than in the area of interviewing.

I've met many people who were the best choice for a job, but they lost job opportunities to less-qualified people. I also fell into this category until I discovered and applied the emotional causes of the buying/hiring decision. After that, I won jobs over others who were far more qualified than me. In the chapter, *Interviewing,* I apply the lessons learned in this book to the art of interviewing. This material was also used in an all-day workshop I've conducted pro bono at churches to assist job seekers.

The final chapter is entitled *Fulfillment*. Whatever your job, your effectiveness and your career fulfillment can be furthered by understanding and applying the emotional causes that produce favorable decisions. By causing favorable buying decisions, hiring decisions, or decisions about a project you've presented to upper management, you can positively impact your financial wellbeing and career success. As this chapter shows, many of the decisions affecting your career are caused by emotions.

We've only begun. We've just cracked the door. Now it is time to broaden our understanding of what causes the buying decision.

2: The Power of Perception

If emotions are the causes of buying decisions, then how do we generate these emotions? One approach is to change the way we, and our product, are perceived, because perceptions can generate powerful feelings.

Perception Is Reality. Really?

Is it true, "Perception is reality"? It's true if we interpret it the following way: Our perceptions of people, things, etc., are not real, but they displace what is actually real, and become our reality. In other words, an individual's perception is their reality. As we shall see, this makes perception more powerful and important than reality.

To understand how perceptions can displace reality let's look at the incarcerated, Ponzi scheme king, Bernard Madoff. If he has a good bone in his body, we have yet to develop an X-Ray machine that can find it. However, he shaped perceptions of both himself and his investment firm to generate the powerful emotion of trust, and this led people to give him their fortunes. He wore the finest clothes, lived a lavish lifestyle, and produced a consistent level of investment returns that were unmatched and unbelievable. He was golden and everything he touched turned to gold. We now know his investing success was a lie, but he created the perception he desired: He was a winner, and investing your money with Madoff enabled you to join his charmed circle of winners.

Now reverse the Madoff image. Imagine someone who is genuinely the world's greatest investor, and a person of perfect integrity. However, he wears filthy jeans with holes in them, and smells like a homeless person. He has a spike through his nose, a tattoo of a gargoyle running up his neck, and cannot look you in the eye. Would you feel safe investing your savings with him? Probably not, because the overwhelming perception he creates is one of strangeness and not of perfect integrity and investing savvy. His outside—what we perceive—does not match his inside.

We base our perceptions on sensory information, primarily on what we see and hear. People choose con men over people of integrity and substance because they cannot look into a person's heart. They can only observe what is presented to them through a person's behaviors. Our behaviors shape perceptions, and these perceptions generate an emotional response.

Changes in our behaviors, our appearance, the things we say and how we say it, change a customer's perception of us. It alters their reality. This changes how they feel about us and affects their buying decision. Therefore, the focus of sales must be on behaviors.

First Impressions And Mindsets

We all know that first impressions are important, but why? Why do they set the tone for the many personal interactions that follow? Why are bad first impressions hard to overcome?

First impressions are essentially mindsets, for they share with the mindset the following characteristics: they are quick to form, resist change,[4] and assimilate all additional information to conform to the existing image.[5]

Mindsets expect to see what they then see. The following exercise helps illustrate this reality-warping power of the mindset. Please

---

[4] Richards J. Heuer, Jr., *Psychology of Intelligence Analysis,* (Center for the Study of Intelligence, CIA, 1999), p. 10. This book is now out of print and this quote comes from the pdf that is available at www.odci.gov/csi.
[5] Heuer, p. 11.

The Power of Perception

look at the following image and answer the question, "What do you see?"

Did you see "Paris in the spring"? Most people do, but the image is "Paris in the *the* spring."

We tend to see the familiar phrase that we *expect* to see, not the phrase that is actually there. Mindsets are more important than reality in a sales situation, because reality tends to conform to the mindset and not the reverse.

The above picture comes from a book written for CIA intelligence analysts. It said the following about the 'Paris in the the spring' picture:

> Did you perceive Figure 1 correctly? If so, you have exceptional powers of observation, were lucky, or have seen the figure before. This simple experiment demonstrates one of the most fundamental principles concerning perception:
>
> **We tend to perceive what we expect to perceive.**[6]

What customers expect to see, they see. *To cause the buying decision we need to create favorable mindsets since they shape what a customer expects to see.* Mindsets are like perceptual filters. And since perceptions generate emotions that cause buying decisions, mindsets become a critical piece of the sales puzzle. Therefore, we need to make mindsets work for us and not against us.

---

[6] Heuer, p. 8.

The Causes of Sales Success

We will first look at mindsets with respect to forming good first impressions. Later on, we will look at the incredible power mindsets have over other areas of our selling activity.

Behavioral Elements Of First Impressions

Meta-Communications

Meta-communications, as I define it, are the things we communicate without saying a word. How we dress is certainly part of this category—and it is covered below—but so is our body language, tone of voice, posture, eye contact, firmness of our handshake, the overpowering scent of too much cologne, etc. All of these meta-communications shape the impression we initially make. Note how the first impression of the world's best investor with the gargoyle tattoo was formed without him saying a word. Had he spoken it is doubtful we would have heard him since his appearance was deafening.

We underestimate the power of these behaviors to form a perception that we in no way want a customer to have. Take, for example, something as simple as the tone of our voice. Our tone and the speed with which we speak, can communicate confidence or anxiety.

I know a person who went through an executive out-placement program, and while answering a question covering a weak area in his background the coach said, "The pitch of your voice just went up." He couldn't tell, and said, "Really?" The coach said, "It happens all of the time. When people speak about a subject that makes them anxious their pitch sometimes betrays their anxiety. Now here's how to handle it." He gave his client some techniques for answering difficult questions and the anxiety went away, as did the change in pitch.

We get anxious when we approach trouble spots in our background, and in our product line, and we can be unconsciously expressing anxiety as we cover these areas. A customer who senses this expression of anxiety will think, "This must really be a huge shortcoming. It even makes him nervous."

Body language is another critical area of meta-communications. Erect posture, eye contact, a smile, a firm handshake communicates confidence. This is obvious, and yet I have seen experienced salespeople slouching in their chair as they spoke to a decision maker. Did it kill the sale? Probably not, but it did diminish the authority of the salesperson who was speaking.

First impressions, and the mindsets they create, do not cause the buying decision; but I have seen them prevent a sale from occurring, so they are important. I knew a friendly, warm-hearted salesperson who was unaware he was creating the impression that he was a jerk, and was barred from entering some hospitals as a result. We will look at his story in the chapter *Sales Performance Coaching*.

Why he remained ignorant of his egregious conduct was the same reason why the slouching salesperson was unaware he was slouching in front of a customer: we cannot observe our selling behaviors as completely and objectively as a sales performance coach can.

People Perceive the Way You Perceive Them

Something as simple as your attention, indicated by the direction of your gaze, can generate positive and negative perceptions and emotions. If you are meeting a group of people, then try to divide your attention equally. Look at everyone every so often. No one wants to feel like they do not merit attention. This behavior of unintentionally ignoring someone can generate a strong emotional response.

Sometimes we may stare at the person who has the highest rank, because we think this will help our cause, only to find out the decision maker was someone else who was also in the room. Oops! Or we can focus our attention on the actual decision maker and make a bad first impression on those who strongly influence the decision. When it comes time to make a decision these powerful influencers may oppose us for reasons they don't entirely understand, they just know they don't want to do business with us.

"The Apparel Oft Proclaims the Man."[7]

(From Polonius' advice to Laertes in *Hamlet*, by William Shakespeare.)

Shakespeare had it right. What we wear has an impact on how we are perceived. But how times have changed since the publication of the book *Dress For Success*, by John T. Molloy (copyright 1975). Suits have disappeared from many workplaces. Blazers and slacks can be too dressy for some venues, or not dressy enough for others.

Based on this, some might come to the dangerous conclusion that what we wear no longer matters. The opposite is true. Attention to what one wears is more important than ever, because there is no longer one dress standard that we can safely follow other than this: wear something similar to what the decision makers are wearing.

I cannot imagine wearing a suit to the Google-plex. It would be as appropriate as wearing a fur coat to a PETA meeting. But if I am giving a high-level presentation to hospital administrators, I cannot imagine wearing anything other than a very good suit. The key to dressing appropriately is to blend in with style. To do otherwise is to disrespect your customer's cultural norms, and this is one of the reasons why our clothes can pack such an emotional punch.

I've met salespeople who believed the quality of their clothing did not matter so they wore suits that looked like they had been re-gifted to the Salvation Army several times. If you are trying to sell the C-level officers of a company a million dollar system, and they are wearing suits that cost over $1,000, then how much have you lowered your chances of success if you look like $10? They will probably wonder if your company will still be in business since you cannot afford to dress better. Or they may think your company is not the sort they want to do business with since its representatives don't even care about their appearance.

---

[7] William Shakespeare, *Hamlet*, Act I, Scene iii, l. 72.

Presentations

Sometimes you meet a dozen or more people for the first time during a presentation. They slowly filter into the room and they observe you and form a first impression of you. Positive or negative mindsets are forming quickly. This is how the mind works and we need to take advantage of this.

One of the things I made sure I would do as the customers arrived was walk up to them, shake their hand and introduce myself. I would thank them for coming, and find out who they were and what they did for their company or hospital. I wanted to project an image of confidence and warmth so I smiled as they told me about themselves.

Sometimes, I'd ask a higher-ranking member of the audience, "Is there anyone I should watch out for?" And this icebreaker would cause a laugh.

Had I paced behind a podium, waiting for the room to fill, would I have been perceived in the same way? I don't think so. Unwelcome thoughts might cross their mind like, "Why is he so nervous, pacing around back there? I guess he realizes he doesn't have a shot at the business. Time to start texting my friends about how bored I am."

Is taking command of the room difficult to do? Yes, because we are often keyed up just moments before a presentation. But for that very reason it becomes more important to act in this way, because it helps differentiate you from the other salespeople who will follow.

Finally, do not overlook the possible use of humor to lighten the mood and help create a positive first impression. However, humor is like a delicious spice. A little bit of it can make the presentation a tasty treat. Too much of it can overwhelm the audience's impression of your product. At the end of a stand-up comedian's presentation, the customer doesn't remember much about his product, but they sure thought he was one funny guy.

Forging Positive Emotional Connections

Mindsets communicate a valuable truth: *when we expect to see something, we see it*, but "perception is affected not only by what people *expect* to see; it is also colored by what they *want* to see."[8]

The question this raises is, "How do we get a customer to want to see us succeed?"

We achieve this end by forging a positive emotional connection with our customers. Once this is accomplished, then everything we say or do is filtered through a favorable lens. For example, if we accidentally misstate a fact the customer will believe we've simply made an honest mistake. But if we are disliked, then our misstatement of fact can turn us into a liar in the customer's mind.

In one instance, the customer wants you to succeed and this desire shapes his perception of you. In the other case, the customer wants you to fail. So we not only need to create positive mindsets of ourselves in the customer's mind, we also need to forge a positive emotional connection. One of the best ways to do this is through entertainment.

Entertainment and Courtship Behaviors

I'll never forget the student who complained that a competitor was buying the business through lavishly entertaining customers. This competitor would fly customers to their manufacturing headquarters and, on arrival, would treat them to a spa experience, to a meal prepared by an on-site chef, to a party with the company's good looking salespeople that went well into the evening, and then to a plant tour the next day.

Now I ask you, "If the decision is rational, then how does having a great time with a company's employees have any influence on what a customer buys? Does this change what their product or service does?" No, the product or service remains the same; however, because the decision is emotional, forging a positive, emotional

---

[8] Scott Plous, *The Psychology of Judgment and Decision Making* (New York: McGraw Hill, 1993), p. 18.

The Power of Perception

connection with your customers has tremendous influence. For the competitor was not merely entertaining the customer by treating them to a casual lunch, he was virtually "courting" her, and courtship behaviors are powerful.

Let's look at "courting" and how an approximation of this works in sales. When a man or woman seeks a committed relationship they often engage in courtship behaviors, that is, they make the other person feel like they are the center of their universe. They go out of their way to please this person in a thoughtful and touching manner, and the emotional power of this approach is demonstrated by the result that often follows: the marriage decision.

This decision may be completely irrational in many cases—e.g., the couple may be totally incompatible on bedrock issues related to friends, family, religion, politics, money, and so on—and yet the marriage decision is made because of the power of courtship behaviors.

Now let's return to the competitor's salespeople whose behaviors resembled courting. They went out of their way to make their customer-group feel like they were the center of this corporation's universe, and every attentive detail increased the impact of this perception-altering experience. From now on, whenever these customers see the salespeople associated with this event, they will likely smile and almost glow inside as they remember their wonderful experience.

Was our competitor buying the customer's business? No. Money, in the form of bribes, was not being passed from our competitor to the customer. But they were applying an emotional cause—courtship behaviors—to generate a buying-decision-effect.

Personally, I am glad to see hospitals and other businesses embracing programs that steer their personnel clear of such attempts at influence, but so long as it was acceptable, and our competitors were using this, we needed to counter it and we did. We designed a better plant-tour/entertainment-program for our customers. (Customers who experienced both plant tours volunteered this assessment to us.) It nullified our competitor's powerful advantage, and through this, and the utilization of other emotional levers, we began to consistently outsell this competitor, who was much larger and had a good reputation. Meanwhile, our small company was virtually unknown to hospitals.[9]

What was the competitor's response to our change? They kept doing the same thing, and failed to adapt, because they were lost in the unlit maze of sales. They had not cracked this code. Our competitor entertained because they knew it worked. But they did not know *why* it worked, or how this knowledge could be applied elsewhere in other ways.

It is critical to forge a positive emotional connection with our decision-making customers. Entertaining is one of the ways this process is accelerated.

Changing the Way You Are Perceived

Here is a rule to live by: *People enjoy buying, but they hate being sold*. If this is true—and it is—then we need to restructure all of our sales and marketing efforts so that they do not appear so sales-y. It is easier to do this than you might think.

For example, during the plant visit we made it a point to never pitch our product in a traditional way. We presented our solutions in stories and focused on the solutions our products offered. This required discussing typical problems hospitals face and discovering specific ones they faced. We would then explore ways our applications might solver their problems.

The powerful thing about a solution-focused approach is the way the salesperson disappears and becomes a member of the customer's

---

[9] Here is a brief story illustrating just how unknown we were. Our company, that I will call Small Midwestern, was located a mere fifteen miles north of Chicago's city center. I was making a presentation to one of the most prestigious university hospital systems in Chicago when a customer interrupted me. They saw our market share slide, and how we were ranked slightly ahead of our much larger competitors. The customer found this difficult to believe. In her honest, forthright words she asked, "If you are the largest, then why haven't any of us ever heard of you?" We were both located in the greater Chicago area and we were unknown.

The Power of Perception

team. After all, the salesperson is doing what the customer is doing: Working to solve a problem. Gone are the customer's fears of a slick sales pitch, because no one seems to be selling.

We would try to fly in all customers to our plant tour the day before so that we could entertain them and forge a positive emotional connection. The next morning we'd go to our plant and showed them our intense commitment to quality and customer service. They would then be escorted to a conference room and they expected to be hit between the eyes with the sales pitch. Sometimes they would say upon sitting down, "Okay. Here it comes." This is what they expected, because they had received this treatment from other companies. But since people enjoy buying and hate being sold we avoided stirring up these negative emotions. Our goal was not to "sell" them; instead, we sought to generate emotions that irresistibly led them to a buying decision.

We would start by reiterating the most powerful sources of annoyance caused by their existing system; we'd then show how our product solved these problems and, when this was the case, how no other product did. We then discussed ways our system could be customized to help with workflow to increase productivity. The presentation was interactive, solution-oriented and engaging. For example, we would ask them how they envisioned customizing the system to solve a problem or improve productivity.

We'd then have lunch and briefly introduce them to our CEO. Then they were driven to the airport for their return home. I remember the departing words of the decision maker for a large piece of business that we won a few days later. Just before she entered the limo to depart she said, "I've been here for two days and you've yet to try and sell me."

I smiled and said, "It's all my fault. Have a great trip home." And I thought to myself, "We've been selling you since our salespeople met you at your airport to fly over here." And we had. But our approach was based on developing powerful emotional causes to generate the buying-decision-effect. This involved employing behaviors that have an impact similar to those involved in courting. It involved generating emotions of hope, trust and even fear. And what augmented its power to cause a buying decision was the way it did not feel like being sold.

Objection: This System Is Manipulative

Before going forward, let me deal with the objection that this approach seems too manipulative, or even dishonest.

First, let's look at the manipulation objection. Aren't all sales approaches manipulative? For that matter, aren't all attempts to lead someone an exercise in manipulation? If I am trying to lead you, I am trying to manipulate you to behave in a way that I desire. If I am trying to sell you, I am trying to manipulate you in a way that results in you buying my product. So, of course it is manipulative.

"Is manipulation inherently wrong?" If it is, then leaders are bad people, even when they are good leaders who are attempting to lead us in the right direction.

"Is *emotional* manipulation inherently wrong?" If emotional manipulation is inherently bad, then countless marriages were the outcome of evil. Courting the one you love and hope to marry is emotional manipulation/selling at its finest.

If your objection is against emotional manipulation, then you are arguing against human nature. Let me know if you win that argument. Emotional manipulation, leadership, persuasion, selling—call it what you will—works because that is how we are wired.

In sales, you have the following choice: You can sell with human nature or against it. Now what do you think your odds of success will be if you try to persuade someone in a way that runs contrary to their nature? If you have strong competitors who are using the same approach, your odds of closing the sale will be about what your market share percentage is. If you have a 30% market share, then you will probably win around three out of ten sales contests.

Now let's change this scenario ever so slightly. What are your odds if you are competing against someone who understands the causes of sales success, and executes them with confidence? Your odds are about the same as climbing to the top of Mount Everest without training, Sherpas or oxygen.

If we fail to influence a customer's emotions when they are making a buying decision involving a significant amount of money, then we will fail to close sales when competing against those who do. That is why this approach can give you an enormous competitive advantage.

Now here is the funny part. You may *feel* ethically superior for refusing to appeal to someone's emotions, but just make sure you realize that your emotions—how you *feel* about this subject—are why you decided to act this way. For you see, everyone—even those who object—are subject to a nature that leads us to make important decisions based on our feelings.

Finally, is the approach dishonest? No. It is scrupulously honest and has to be. The foundation of this approach is developing a bond of trust, and the last time I checked this was more likely to occur when someone was, and is, scrupulously honest.

The only thing that separates great salespeople from great con artists is integrity. They both use many of the same techniques to sell people, because their techniques are aligned with human nature. They are like an arsonist and a master chef who both use fire. The fire is morally neutral, but the individuals using it are not. So, it is with ethical salespeople and con artists. Neither is responsible for the way human nature operates, but they are morally responsible for how they utilize this knowledge.

The Next Two Chapters

Perceptions are powerful and they are formed by our appearance and our behaviors. In the next two chapters we will look at some of the behaviors we can employ to change a customer's perception.

1. Ask custom-tailored questions.

2. Adopt a consultative sales style.

3: Power Questions

I'll never forget the Chief Nursing Officer's (CNO) statement to me as we were enjoying dinner with her key staff members. She said, "You really surprised me over the phone." I gave her a puzzled look and asked, "Uh oh. What did I do now?"

"Well you told me that you wanted to ask some questions to get an idea about some of the issues and problems we might be facing prior to our visit, and I thought, 'Oh boy, here comes the questions about how important is this feature and that feature.' You know, the standard sales routine. But you asked me questions about my goals, my vision for the nursing department and I was stunned."

"Is that a good thing or a bad thing?" I asked.

She smiled and said, "It's a good thing. I found it refreshing."

Almost every sales book tells you to ask questions, but as the CNO's response indicates, sometimes these questions can generate a negative perception of the salesperson. What is important, therefore, is not asking the typical salesperson questions, but asking ones that favorably change a customer's perception of you.

I've literally seen a salesperson's career go from being a slow-moving train wreck to being a rewarding profession by doing one thing: Asking relevant, custom-tailored questions. His story follows.

The Power of Asking Good Questions

I was working for a distributor of commodity packaging products and the margins were razor thin. This required every salesperson to produce and one of them wasn't. He was a friendly sort, and smart enough to be a successful salesperson, only he wasn't succeeding. So, I traveled with him to see what it was he would say to his prospects and accounts. He would typically start a sales call by asking:

> Hey Joe, got anything for me to bid on today?

He thought he was serving his company well, beating the bushes, trying to uncover some opportunities, and did not realize this question was killing whatever chances he may have had to succeed.

At first, the question seems harmless, but when we consider it from the customer's perspective, it is anything but. The salesperson thought he was communicating:

> Hey Joe, throw me a bone and I will see if I can shave off a few nickels to save you some money to make you look good.

He didn't realize he was actually saying:

> Hey Joe, you can probably imagine that since I'm traveling with my boss I need to close some business. Any business. Yes, if you throw me a bone it will create work for you, and the savings I will be able to offer are probably insignificant, and what you've got is probably working fine, but still, you gotta help me. Please!

After two performances like this I'd seen enough. The next account we were visiting was a division of 3M. I had to give the kid credit for at least scheduling an appointment that looked like it had potential, but the last thing we needed was one of his repeat performances in front of a professional outfit of their caliber. So, I took him off to the side and made him rehearse a few questions with me, repeatedly, until he memorized them. Then I said, "After our introductions I want you to lead off with these questions."

They were targeted questions that were related to potential problems they might be having with packaging that led to the quarantining of product. *Do you often quarantine products because of packaging defects? Was this quarantining of products a big problem?*

After he asked these questions, and a few others we had rehearsed, the engineer turned from the salesperson to me and said, "No one has ever asked me those questions before." He looked back at the salesperson, "Look, the person you need to see is so and so. Talk to him about this and tell him I sent you."

Why such a strong response? Because we were probably the first company to ask this engineer questions designed to uncover problems relevant to him. Would a question about a packaging problem affect a CEO so powerfully? Only if he had experienced a packaging problem so large in scale that it threatened quarterly earnings, or the company's quality reputation in the marketplace. But for this engineer packaging was a big deal. His response confirmed this fact. This is why questions need to be custom-tailored.

The salesperson who asked, "Hey Joe, you got anything for me to bid on today?" was the same salesperson who asked consultative questions to an engineer working for a Fortune 500 company, and who then grew his business by 30% that year. In other words, the problem was not with who the salesperson was, but with his behaviors. Once the behaviors changed (in this case, *questions*), the results were completely different.

Few things have the ability to change a customer's perception of a salesperson as completely as informed and targeted questions do. They also uncover what is emotionally important to the customer and this makes effective questioning critical.

The Best Questions

The best questions are the ones that reveal powerful emotional responses. A question I always asked everyone, regardless of their rank, was, "What are your goals?" After they answered this general question I would follow up with a more specific question, "What goals has your boss tasked you to accomplish? Are they same as the ones you've just shared?"

There are two primary reasons why these questions are powerful. First, our goals are tied to the powerful emotion of hope. What does the customer *hope* to accomplish this year? Second, a boss's goals are typically tied to incentive pay or rewards. Since money is emotion quantified, and emotions cause the buying decision, uncovering a person's incentive-related goals gives you incredibly powerful information. It enables you to show someone how your product or service can help her, and her company, achieve annual goals that enrich both parties. Would this exert an influence over her decision? I think it might.

Bad Questions Can Mislead

Few questions are as universal as, "What are your goals?" Many questions that work at one level in an organization fail at another, and the wrong type of question can sometimes produce misleading information.

For example, let's say your investigation has uncovered the importance of shareholder value to your customer. You've heard this from the lips of both the CFO and CEO when they were responding to questions during a quarterly earnings report conference call.

Now I'm certain the CEO, COO and CFO would all agree that shareholder value was and is important; however, as you move down the org chart these macro issues lose their emotional resonance. Is shareholder value important to the director who is short-staffed, subject to a hiring freeze, and doing the work of three people for his company? Wall Street and the investment community love head count reductions, and frequently greet news of one by boosting a company's share price, but is the overworked director as thrilled about these stock-boosting changes?

If you were to ask this director, "Is shareholder value important to you?" The answer you are likely to get is, "Of course its important." But this could be someone maintaining the company line. This director might fear his real opinion might somehow reach the C-level suite and become a dreaded CLM (Career-Limiting Move).

The problem with the question and its answer is the way it misleads. Imagine this director is the decision maker for your product and you base your presentation on this "need" you've uncovered, and how your product delivers the best shareholder value and return on investment of any product of its type. Will such a presentation, devoid of emotional power, cause a favorable buying decision? That is doubtful. In fact, such a presentation might stir up negative emotions of resentment since macro-issues, like shareholder value, are forcing your decision maker to work like a galley slave.

There is a way to avoid these questioning pitfalls and that is by taking the steps outlined below.

Step One: Develop the Customer Profile

The first step in the process is to develop individual profiles of the decision maker and decision influencers. What are their jobs and responsibilities? What are their typical concerns? What are their biggest problems?

For example, if the Chief Information Officer (CIO) is a decision maker then you know, or can easily find out, that among his likely concerns are the security and stability of the network, cost reduction, productivity enhancement, and so on. If you are unfamiliar with their responsibilities and concerns, then the Internet can provide this information. Simply search "top CIO concerns" and you will get a mountain of feedback. You can filter this further by specifying the industry, the state, etc. If you've been working in the same field for a while, then your experience should enable you to fill out this profile.

Also, if your company has a CIO, try to get an hour of his time during lunch to ask him questions and understand his world from an emotional perspective. What does he fear? What does he think our CIO customers likely fear when they are purchasing our product, or a competitive product? What are his goals or hopes?

These conversations can produce priceless information. I remember speaking to the head of our company's IT department and finding out our CIO customers were fearful about making a purchase of a large system like ours, and then have it fail to produce any of the productivity gains they promised would occur. This fear was

Power Questions

reinforced by the high turnover rate of CIOs at the time. This led us to put greater emphasis during presentations on our installation process, and how we would help them drive the necessary behavior changes in the end-users to produce the productivity gain.

Step one is completed when you develop a list of concerns and problems faced by this particular customer. A partial list of a CIO's likely concerns/interests might look like this:

1. Ensuring the network has the capacity to handle large amounts of traffic.
2. Protecting the security of the network.
3. New products should follow existing standards—be it a fire alarm system, security system, etc.—to prevent the addition of separate networks requiring their own back-up systems, maintenance schedule, etc.

One of these areas of concern could be a failed installation. If a customer has purchased a software program for their network that never delivered on its promise, and it was de-installed, then he will likely be interested in training programs, support, and so on.

You can add to your list:

4. De-installs.
5. Training programs that make de-installs less likely, etc.

It is important to find out industry specific concerns so you are able to show you understand their unique needs. For example, hospital CIOs may have unique needs centered on Electronic Medical Record development. Being conversant in these specific subjects, and asking insightful questions about them, can change a customer's perception of the salesperson. It can make him appear to be a member of the team, a consultant who is helping them solve problems.

Also, issues specific to the organization they work for will have a major impact on their responsibilities and concerns. The CEO may have tasked the CIO with transformational goals driven by the innovative use of information to improve decision-making. One never knows how the leadership in an organization will give an enterprise a unique focus, but the salesperson needs to find this out.

Step Two: Match Solutions to Concerns

We marry the primary benefits of the product to the concerns of the customer in the second stage. You go down the list of their concerns and say, "For this concern we offer this solution. And for this concern we offer that solution." And down the list you go writing down the solutions that fit the best and are the most powerful.

For example, protection against the occurrence of de-installs was a concern, and your product offers the following characteristics or solutions that address this concern:

- Your product has never been de-installed, while all competitive products have.

- The reason for your success is the package of training that comes with the install. The hours allotted for training are 40% more than your next closest competitor.

At the risk of being obvious… There will likely be several concerns your product does not address, or addresses in a weak and inadequate way. After all, no product can do everything. If this is the case, then questions need not be developed for those concerns.

Step Three: Develop Questions

Next, we develop questions that validate the strength of these concerns. Let's return to the suspected concern about de-installs. It leads us to develop the following question:

> Have you ever experienced a software de-install and is it a concern?

This question wants to discover if this is an area that either elicits a pained response or no response. If they have experienced a de-install, then it is likely they want to avoid going through it again. But they may try to conceal their emotional reaction to the question and simply offer a tight-lipped, "Yes. I've experienced a de-install."

The following is critical. The questions you have on a sheet of paper may not produce all of the information you need, but the follow-up questions typically do. Therefore, you do not go on to the next question until you understand how strong or weak their emotional response is to this question. You must continue to burrow deeper with potential questions like:

> How did that process go for you?
>
> Was it costly?
>
> What went wrong?

If they answer, "I'd rather not relive that experience." Then you will know this was an emotional experience worth addressing during your presentation.

I've found that in most instances customers are quite free to share their bad experiences, because they don't want to relive them in the future. Listening to your solution may provide them with a much-desired sense of relief.

Customers are also more likely to speak freely when you preface your questions with the following promise:

> I understand you are going to be attending the presentation this Friday, is that correct? Great. To make this presentation relevant to you and your department, I'd like to ask you a few questions to find out what some of your concerns are. If I know what they are, then I can speak about how our product addresses these concerns.
>
> For example, have you ever experienced a software de-install and is it a concern?

Note: I've stated the reason why I am asking him questions in a way that focuses on his benefit. If he answers my questions, then at least one of the long presentations he has to sit through will address some of his concerns. It's like saying, "Give me a moment of your time so that I don't completely waste your time on Friday."

Also, I don't ask his permission to ask questions. I don't ask if he has time to answer them right now—because this may be my only chance to ask them. Instead, I launch into the first question as a way of showing how they will be relevant to his concerns.

That said, if I see him fidgeting or looking at his watch, then I ask if there is a better time to conduct this survey, and that it will be brief. Someone who is visibly distracted is a bad candidate for questions. Their mind is elsewhere, perhaps on a meeting they are already late to attend. Since I want to create the mindset that I am a consultant who works for them, and is part of their team, I cannot allow my behaviors to undermine this by acting like a pushy salesperson.

Step Four: Test the Acceptability of Your Solution

You've now discovered an emotionally hot area and you have a product solution that fits it. Why do I need to test whether or not they value our solution? It's our solution...what else am I going to present? The following example illustrates the importance of this step.

There was a hospital trying to improve the patient's experience. Also, due to a nursing shortage, they were looking for ways to make nurses more productive and remove unnecessary steps.

It just so happened that there was a perfect solution to their problem: A wireless phone network. When a patient called for help a phone-carrying technical assistant could answer to find out what was needed. The patient might say, "I need a blanket." Now the tech could go get the blanket and deliver it rather than walk to the room, find out what is needed, walk to get the blanket, and then walk back to the room. The patient's call would be answered more quickly, and the need was taken care of with fewer steps being taken. Patient satisfaction scores rise, unnecessary steps are removed... it's perfect!

It's presentation time. You are so amped you can barely control yourself. You now remind the account of their goals, present your solution, and the nurses respond. "I don't want a phone to interrupt me when I am trying to take care of a patient." Another stirs up the emotion of fear: "What if the phone rings, it is a patient in distress,

Power Questions

and I am changing a wound dressing? The patient dies, and the phone log shows I failed to answer their call, because I couldn't. Phone system? No way."

This is why you test a solution first. It can keep you from walking into a buzz saw. If you know the concerns your solution generates, you can either deal with them upfront, or focus on other solutions.

We return to the de-install example to show how this stage of the questioning is handled:

> We share your concern about de-installs. We are the only company in our space that has no de-installs and the reason why is we offer a comprehensive training program that makes de-installs far less likely. *Would you like me to cover that during the presentation?*
>
> He responds, "In detail. And I want you to explain to the people why it is critically important that they all participate in this training, because if they don't, we all lose."

The strength of the response let's you see how emotionally important the solution is. Since he wants you to cover your installation process in detail, you will need to make it interesting. The key is to use repetition with variation, repeating the same solution in different ways. We will cover this technique of repetition with variation in several of the following chapters.

Follow-Up Questions and Notes

Follow-up questions are vital to the success of your consultative questioning. The first question sometimes generates a meaningful response, but we shouldn't be satisfied with it. For example, let's say you ask, "Have you ever experienced a software de-install and is it a concern?" And the CIO answers, "Yeah I've been through a de-install, and it got me de-installed. So I'd say it was important."

This is valuable information and, by itself, it might be all you need to craft a solution that wins the sale. But why not probe a little more deeply? The follow-up questions are often the ones that unlock the door to sales success. So you ask, "What's the worst thing about a de-install?"

The CIO answers:

> It's like throwing away hundreds of invested man-hours. Time is our most precious commodity and we will never get back all of that wasted time.

Memorable phrases from decision makers are like diamonds from a mine. These words are the product of enormous pressure and they are extremely valuable. Be sure you write down answers like this word for word, because when it comes time to present the product you can say the following:

> Our product has never been de-installed. None of our competitors can say this. If you choose our system, you won't need to worry about *throwing away hundreds of invested man-hours*. This is critical, because *time is our most precious commodity*. And the time you lose from a de-install is time you *will never get back*.

The italicized words came directly from the CIO's mouth. As you repeat his words, you will see him furiously nodding his head up and down. It is like you are speaking directly to his soul. "He gets it!" this person's mind will shout. It will seem like you are reading his mind, because you are literally giving voice to his thoughts. When we speak a decision maker's own words back to an audience that they are a part of, it is as if we have publicly validated what they have believed for years. Is that emotionally powerful? Oh yes.

If a customer says something memorable and emotion-laden do not bring attention to it by saying something like, "That's great stuff." Or, "Do you mind if I use that." Simply write it down and use it during your next presentation.

Framing the Question

How you ask questions can shape the customer's perception of you. For example, you have identified network security as an area of

Power Questions

customer concern and interest, so you ask, "Is network security important for you?"

This question is unfortunate in that it successfully targets a concern, but in a way that makes you look like you have no clue what his CIO-world is like. He might think, dismissively, "Of course it's important. Does this guy know anything?" And then he might say, "Network security is important to everyone," to mask his disdain ever so slightly.

Since the goal is to generate positive perceptions and emotions it is important to frame questions in a way that reveals an understanding of their profession. Another way to ask the same question is, "You have to juggle many priorities. Is network security your highest priority or does anything outrank it?"

From the Particular to the General

By asking questions that reveal your understanding of the decision maker's world and their needs, you will create the perception that you are not a salesperson, but a consultant who is trying to uncover problems and implement solutions. With that mindset established the customer is more likely to share things openly with you. Now you can ask general questions designed to uncover emotionally important areas that your targeted questions may have missed. For example, "What do you most fear occurring to your company or to your department?"

I remember a hospital administrator telling me, "Losing one of our busiest surgeons to a competitive hospital. If he walks away, then $12 million in annual revenue walks away with him." Up until the time I heard that answer I'd never thought about giving emphasis to the way our system improved the satisfaction of surgeons and physicians throughout the hospital since it was a system used primarily by nurses.

Another general question that they have probably never been asked by anyone before is, "What are the things that you do in your job that you enjoy the most, that you are most passionate about?" If you can uncover the sources of joy in someone's oftentimes joyless job, and show how your product allows them to tap into that area of passion, you will not only improve your chances of winning the customer's business, you will also be on your way to developing an important business friendship.

No Karnaks Need Apply

The late Johnny Carson used to perform a comedy sketch wherein he became Karnak the Magnificent. (His work, though long gone, can still be found on YouTube.) Karnak had the amazing ability to know the answer to any question before the question was asked. To demonstrate this power he would hold an envelope to his head. In the envelope was the question. He would then announce the answer to the question before opening the envelope. For example, he might say the following answer, "Catch 22." Then he would open the envelope and read the question, "What would the Dodgers do if you hit 100 pop flies?"

In sales, there are no Karnaks. The answer comes after the question, not before, and once we assume we know the answer to a given question, we are preparing ourselves to receive an unhappy surprise. I experienced this first hand in Napa Valley.

We visited a hospital and gave a presentation based on how our product helped retain nurses by supplying them with the resources they needed to meet the demands of their job. This presentation had delivered us many purchase orders. It was resonating with customers because the nursing shortage was real at the time, and causing concern among hospitals. So we kept banging that bell—nursing shortage, nursing shortage—until finally the nurse interrupted us and said, "We don't have a nursing shortage here. I've got a list of people who are waiting for openings so they can join us. I don't know what its like elsewhere, but this is Napa."

"Hey Karnak," I thought as I kicked myself, "there is no benefit, perceived or real, when you pitch a solution to a customer that they don't need."

I share this humbling story so that you might remember to never assume you know the answer to the unasked question. Karnak was a great entertainer, but a lousy salesperson.

Conclusion

The causes of the buying decision are emotional, and we are in the process of realigning everything we do in sales to reflect this understanding. These questions, often referred to as a *needs analysis*, are no longer an attempt to find out what their business supposedly needs. Instead, it is an attempt to find out what emotionally moves decision makers the most powerfully.

Needs analysis has always been an important exercise, because one's needs have an emotional component. But we improve this analysis by applying our understanding of the emotional causes of the buying-decision-effect. Instead of trying to discover "needs," we search for emotions like hope, fear, and joy. Needs analysis does not do this by design. If it did, then some of the questions I've introduced, "What are your goals?" and, "What are you passionate about in your work?" would be questions that are routinely asked. But they aren't, and that is because we have tended to approach sales as if it was a rational process, when it is not.

Asking customized questions is what a consultant does. In the next chapter, we will look at another side of the consultative sales process.

4: Consultative Selling

What Purpose Does a Consultant Serve?

Why are consultants hired?

We were selling a big-ticket item and oftentimes found ourselves selling both to a consultant and to the customer. Why? What purpose did this consultant serve?

When a customer is buying a complex product or service—e.g., a telecommunications system, a corporation-wide software program, etc.—and its operation is outside their expertise, they will often hire a consultant to fill in the knowledge gap. They *fear* making a mistake, so they turn to an outside expert to help them make the right decision.

This fear that drives customers into the arms of consultants is real, because the price of a bad decision can be high. For example, let's say I have a budget of $1 million for some much-needed telecommunications gear, and I buy a system that lasts one year. The short shelf life of my purchase was caused by my company's expansion, and the inability of my chosen system to expand with us. A year after spending $1 million, our company now has to spend another million to get a new system that will grow with them. Ouch!

Had I made this purchasing mistake would I be allowed to make the decision about its replacement? That's very doubtful. More than likely, *my replacement* would be given the authority to make the next decision and, to avoid my fate, she would bring in experts to help her steer clear of the many traps a complex system can have.

Fear. Few emotions are more powerful. When we realize the consultant's role is to remove fear from the decision-making process we begin to understand what a consultative salesperson's role should be. She is the expert in the product or service she represents, and the customer is not. Instead of selling the customer, the consultative salesperson's role is to help them make the emotional migration from fear (what if we make a bad decision?), to trust (your solution is acceptable), to partnership (we've bought your product).

When a customer must spend thousands of dollars on a piece of equipment they naturally fear making the wrong choice, and their fears are not just product related. They also extend to the company and salesperson representing the product. The consultative sales approach knows it must address these fears so that the customer and salesperson can successfully enter into a satisfying partnership.

Product Fears

As Apple, Inc. taught the world, consumers love simple, intuitive products. Therefore, Apple designs products that require no training manual. This design philosophy was a major factor in their becoming the most highly valued company in the world.

It is likely that your product does not enjoy the benefit of Apple's brand recognition. So, even if you have a genuinely simple product (this is reality), the customer may still see it as being too complex (perception trumps reality). When you look at your product you see something you are familiar with, but your customer sees something alien, a product requiring training and adding complexity to their lives.

Complexity generates feelings of unease and fear. With the exception of self-destructive people, no one seeks to complicate their life needlessly. Because of this, if there was one fear I always tackled head on, whether I was speaking with end-users or administrative decision makers, it was the fear of complexity.

The Causes of Sales Success

There are many ways to demonstrate a product's simplicity, but the one I found to be the most effective was asking customers who the most technologically challenged member of their group was. Ask it with a smile and it becomes a fun game for them to decide, and it usually doesn't take long. The technologically challenged typically have a reputation that they are almost proud of. He will either raise his hand or their colleagues will quickly point him out.

Next, I would ask this person, "Would you be kind enough to participate in a product demonstration? The reason why I am asking you is simple. Customers want simple, easy-to-use products. Salespeople live with their products, so they can always make a product look simple, even when it's not. But if I can get you to use this product without much training, then it probably is easy to use." Then I motion to a chair and say, "Please." I've never had a customer say no.

Every product has some complexity, but if it is well designed, then its basic functionality is straightforward. So walking a technophobe through the demo is not difficult. I would keep this part of the demonstration short and basic. I would also cover the tasks that they would likely perform several times a day or week. For example, how do you sign into the system and how do you sign out. Then, when this demonstration was finished, I'd ask his colleagues to give him a round of applause, and the mood of the room was brightened for the rest of the presentation.

There are other product fears and these are typically uncovered when we ask our custom-tailored questions. Whatever they are, they need to be addressed. But two fears that often get overlooked involve the relationship that a purchase entails. Is your company reliable, ethical, and likely to be in business several years down the road? Are you, the salesperson, ethical, reliable, and committed to giving excellent service.

If you work for a bad company, or if you are a bad salesperson, then the product can be great but the customer experience can be one of unending pain and suffering. For this reason, these fears also need to be addressed if the consultative salesperson is ever to bring the customer to the point of trust and partnership.

Company Fears

Are you a small company competing against giants? When you work for a small company, and there are big-company alternatives, the spoken or unspoken fears are, "Do they have the resources and the wherewithal to sustain product development and stay current with this rapidly-changing world? And will they be around five years from now to service our purchase?"

Turn this fear on its head by making this perceived weakness a significant strength. I would tell customers visiting our corporate headquarters the following:

> What name is synonymous with searching the Internet? Google. If you think back far enough, Google was once a tiny little gnat compared to Yahoo, Microsoft and AOL-Time Warner. But in the game of Internet search, it crushed its much larger competitors. Why? Because Google focused on this one thing, searching the Internet, and did it better than anyone else. We are also small compared to our competitors, but we are totally focused on the system you are considering.
>
> However, this system's revenue barely appears on our competitor's balance sheets. Do an automated word search of their annual reports and see if this product category is even mentioned. It isn't. This product is virtually invisible to our big competitors. But for us, it is what we do, and that's why we are the best at it.

The above introduces the subject of differentiation. It is the art of comparing your product, company, etc., to your competitors, in a favorable way. In the above, we not only make our small size our strength, but their large size a great weakness. The message is: this product line is so insignificant to them they pay it little attention.

Objections to Differentiation

I do not see how one can sell in a consultative way without differentiating. Isn't that what a consultant does? Do they not advise their customers about the differences between the products they are considering?

The Causes of Sales Success

To the above assertion you may respond: "But how can I be the customer's consultant when I am biased for my product and they know I am biased for my product?"

Easy. All consultants are biased. In fact, they are among some of the most biased people I've ever dealt with. They all tended to favor certain solutions over other ones, even when those choices were ultimately bad for their client. I've witnessed their biased recommendations result in the installation of vastly inferior systems that were de-installed after only three traumatic and unhappy years. Normally this system should have lasted for at least ten years.

You are no different from "real" consultants when it comes to being biased. Therefore, when you behave like a consultant you will soon be perceived as one. And you *will* be one if you deliver valuable consulting advice that reveals to your customer the shortcomings of other product choices and the strengths of your own.

Think about it. If the customer does not know how the systems differ from each other, how can they make an informed decision? And if I believe my system is far superior—I did—and I fail to make this case strongly enough, and the customer ends up buying an inferior system, then we both lose.

If differentiation offends, then it should never be practiced. One should never speak in an emotionally offensive way. But it doesn't offend when done properly. During my presentations, I would speak about our competitors continually, even when the customer loved our competitor and hated us, and I would, more often than not, end up securing the purchase order.

When I differentiated our product to neutral customers, I would frequently have them come up and thank me after the presentation, because of the way I shared valuable information in a fair way. Knowing the differences between the two products helped them to make a good buying decision that—amazingly enough—just so happened to favor our company's system.

When it comes to how the sales profession typically thinks about differentiation, I am reminded of physicians who bled their patients. In both cases wrongheaded notions were, and are, the order of the day. I've heard the following mantra since my first day of sales training: "Don't talk about the competitor." "Take the high road. Be professional."

What a lot of hooey. If differentiating causes sales to close—and it does—and my job is to close sales, then why should I bow down to the accepted wisdom that is foolish and not wise? The reason why this notion—don't talk about the competitor—took root is because differentiation typically caused more harm than good. In other words, it was done poorly and it generated negative feelings. But when done correctly, differentiation does not offend even the most hostile customer. If the toughest critics do not disapprove, then how can it be unprofessional?

When accepted wisdom is obviously incorrect, then it needs to be dismissed rather than followed. Differentiate. It's what consultants do; and when you act like a consultant, the customer will begin to perceive you are one.

Salesperson Fears

One of the biggest fears a customer can have is also the easiest one to control. If they do not know you, they may distrust you and question everything you say. Therefore, to establish a bond of trust follow this simple set of rules:

1. Always be honest in what you do or say. If you are ever caught in a lie, or a blatant misrepresentation, then you have damaged your relationship with this customer for months, years, perhaps forever.

2. The customer doesn't care to know you until they know you care. Yeah, I know, this sappy truism can generate cringes, but it happens to be true when applied to the world of sales. Make an emotional commitment to always be there for the customer. If they need something—information, a part, some troubleshooting help—fill this need as fast as possible. Move heaven and earth if you must. If they call you and you cannot answer, then make sure you return their call in minutes not hours.

3. Invest the time it takes to understand their world. Consultants do this when they are working on a project for a client.

4. Never be afraid to admit you do not know an answer to a customer's question. To be trusted requires a transparency and honesty that shines through. However, it is up to you to get that answer for them ASAP.

5. Some salespeople use their strong relationships with customers to charge them the highest prices. They do this because they believe they can get away with it, and many do. But if you want to develop a genuine, trusting relationship, then you need to approach customers differently. Your margins and pricing are proprietary pieces of information, but price your product in a way that would stand up to your customer's scrutiny if they were able to examine your books. There is a big difference between being profitable and gouging.

One of our primary sales goals is to create a bond of trust that is both perceived and real. How do consultants approach this subject of trust with a potential customer whose business they are seeking? First, they establish a rapport with their prospect, and then they provide evidence of their trustworthiness. The prospect is provided with references from satisfied customers, letters of recommendation, and the like.

Salespeople should also be able to provide references and testimonials from satisfied customers. These can be included in the Request For Information packet that is often delivered to the customer before the product presentations. Steps like these are designed to accelerate the emotional migration process that moves from fear to trust. If you do this, and your competition doesn't, will this help tip the emotional scales in your favor? Yes.

Humor

Trust. The word has a heavy connotation like the word *stolid*. But being relentlessly serious is no way to build a strong relationship. Customers will find ways to avoid the company of someone who is no fun to be around. So one of the ways to lighten the mood, and grow closer to a customer, is to use humor. It can even be built into your sales process.

We had a VP of Manufacturing who looked menacing. He was massive. It was rumored he had a neck, but the way his head fused to his torso proved the rumor was false. His head sported a Prussian buzz cut. His piercing blue eyes had an intensity that would have made him a great interrogator. And at every opportunity, I would ask him to lead the plant tours.

He would appear in the room where we conducted our presentations and would quietly stand off to the side and look threatening. He wasn't trying to look intimidating, he just did. I would then say, "I'd like to introduce our VP of Manufacturing. Some people are hired for their competence. Others are hired for their looks. You see this when you go to conventions where manufacturers show their gear. They always have face-guys and face-girls at their booths. Our VP of Manufacturing is a face guy."

Though I had said this many times, he would always smile and erupt in laughter—the menacing look would melt away—and he'd say, "Yeah, I'm a face guy. Are you folks ready for our plant tour?" Again, humor is a wonderful spice that can set a positive tone for an experience.

The "Rational" Buying Process

One thing that always amused me about the multi-step complex-sales process was the way it tried to engineer emotion out of the equation. It attempts to be rational and objective at every step. Sometimes end-users were given surveys to fill out during and after presentations, entertainment was forbidden, and time was built into the schedule to allow for deliberation. No rash decisions here!

Unfortunately, there is a problem with this approach: Emotion cannot be engineered out of the process, because ultimately a decision must be made. Since that decision can have good or bad consequences, emotions like fear will always be present. No matter what process a customer puts in place, emotion will always attend buying decisions involving a decent sum of money, because money is emotion quantified.

That said, if a detailed process is in place, then make sure you find the answers to these questions:

1. What are the stages of their process and the dates?//
2. Who is running the process, and is this person my primary point of contact?
3. Are there any special rules, like disqualifying a vendor if they try to speak to members on the decision-making committee?
4. How will the decision be made? For example, will a committee make it immediately after the final presentation?
5. Will there be site visits to see the actual product/service in use?
6. Will there be plant tours?
7. How many presentations will be required and how long will they be?

Once you have the answers, it is important that each step is prepared for and handled in a competent manner. If, for example, you bungle a site visit, or fail to submit requested information by the deadline, then you are damaging the bond of trust you are trying to form. We tend to trust reliable, competent people, and this is why it is critical to master the entire complex-sales process.

Always Advance the Sales Process

A consultative approach to selling should demonstrate a competence that inspires confidence and leads to trust. One of the simplest tools to help manage one or more projects is to always make sure they have a next step and a date.

If you are selling wooden pencils, then you go for the close at every opportunity. But a complex sale is advanced by increments. And, until it is closed, it is easy to lose sight of the fact that there are concrete interim steps you can take to keep advancing the sale.

Consultative Selling

This means that until the sale is closed, and the customer is in-serviced and satisfied, you will always have a next step with a date attached to it. If your manager is not asking you what the next step and date are for an important sales opportunity, then you need to be asking yourself.

Even the final stages of a large sale require attention. For example, let's say you've just finished your final presentation along with your competitors, and the word from the committee is they will get in touch with you in one week with the answer. Your next step and date might be to handwrite on nice stationery a note of thanks to all who attended, and to let them know you are available at all times to answer any lingering questions they may have.

Once the note is mailed, your next step and date is to call the customer the day after the decision was to be announced, if an announcement was not made. This is important. The last thing you want to experience is losing the sale to a salesperson who is more persistent than you during a time when a dithering customer was indecisive. If, for example, I am the only salesperson who fails to follow up with the customer, then it will look like I am not hungry for their business, and will probably not pay much attention to them once the deal is closed. It could be something this small and simple that neutralizes weeks or months of work. And it is so easy to overlook unless you have a next step and a date.

Who Is the Decision Maker?

One of the ways the customer tries to keep the decision making process as rational as possible is by keeping the decision maker hidden. By keeping this information secret, the customer attempts to shield the decision maker from appeals aimed at his specific needs and wants.

However, once the presentation begins the decision maker will often appear in bold relief. Everyone tends to defer to this person. Then, once you know who this person is, be certain to make note of his questions and what seems most important to him.

Here is a rule that should be in effect at every presentation. Whoever is presenting should focus only on presenting. Whoever else is in the room—and when possible, there should always be at least one other person—focuses on the audience. It is difficult to pick up on all of the subtle meta-communications an audience is transmitting while you are focusing on what you are going to say. However, an observer cannot only locate the decision maker, she can also determine how others interact with this person. This can help reveal who the key influencers are. Does the decision maker typically look at one person after saying something? Do they both nod their heads toward each other after making a point, signifying how they agree? Once you know the decision maker and the key influencers, then you know whose emotional needs and wants you will focus on in subsequent presentations.

The Consultant Mindset

We need to change our mindset regarding ourselves, because it is limiting and self-defeating. If you think you are a salesperson, then you will act like a salesperson. And if you think you are a consultant, then you will act like a consultant.

Personally, I've loved being in sales and I enjoy being in the company of salespeople. However, the behaviors associated with a consultant close sales more effectively than those associated with a salesperson. And these consultative behaviors come naturally to the person who thinks he is one.

Adopt behaviors used by consultants: Ask custom-tailored questions, test the adequacy of solutions, present your credentials, differentiate, and note the customer's needs and fears. The solution you provide that addresses these fears will help your customers make the emotional migration from fear to trust. They will hear your presentation and think, "She gets it." As a result, they will want to do business with you. The salesperson is no longer seen as someone pushing a product, but a person possessing specialized knowledge who is part of the customer's team.

One word of advice: Based on the way our minds are wired, do all of the above, and do it before anyone else. Why it's critical to be first is covered in the next chapter.

5: To Be First Is…

To Be First Is… to Finish First

When I analyzed some of our largest business losses, I discovered the following: It was typically due to us being late to the party. Finding an opportunity first confers powerful advantages; therefore, it is critical to be the first person at the scene of the sale.

The Advantage of Being First

Here is what can happen when a talented salesperson, named Susan, finds an opportunity that remains unknown to her competitors.

First, she determines the lay of the land. Who is the decision maker and who are the decision influencers? Once she discovers this, she begins to change their perception of her. Initially they saw a salesperson, but her behaviors transform her into a consultant who works for them.

She asks them about their planned purchase and the process they plan on using. She asks them custom-tailored questions to determine what needs and wants are the most emotionally powerful. She doesn't act like other salespeople. She knows her stuff and literally becomes part of the product-planning committee.

Based on the information her questions uncover, and on the strengths of her product versus the competition, she begins to teach them what is truly important about the product they are planning on buying. In short, she is creating a mindset about the product's specifications that favors her product and tilts the field against her competitors.

In this instance, she closes them on the sale and this opportunity never hits the street, or goes out to bid. But let's assume it did. Once the competition finds out about the opportunity they are confronted with a schedule that gives them little time to prepare. They are never able to secure an advance meeting with the customer—who does not want to meet with them—and do not know who will be making the decision. They have no idea what the "hot buttons" are, and do not realize their product is viewed as being inadequate in the key areas that Susan told them were the most important. Though the product is subjected to the bid process, it is really a formality, because the decision has been made.

By being first to an account a salesperson can start accruing numerous, powerful advantages. No wonder most of our big losses were due to arriving late to the party. Sometimes we were able to overcome these disadvantages, but other times we were not. Therefore, it is essential for a salesperson to include prospecting—hunting for opportunities—in their sales activities. But the last thing we want to do is waste a salesperson's time, so it helps to illustrate what ineffective and effective prospecting looks like.

Ineffective Prospecting

Ineffective prospecting is a blind squirrel finding an acorn every now and then. It looks like this:

> A salesperson gets in her car and drives from account to account where they are not doing business, and asks a few questions to see if there is anything cooking at these accounts. "Hi, I'm Jane Zane from XYZ, Inc. Are you in the market for a new, state-of-the-art whatchamacallit?"

This approach can, on rare occasions, uncover an opportunity, but for the most part, it is a frustrating exercise in futility. After all, what you are attempting to do only enriches you and not the customer who, therefore, views you as a waste of their time. We need to change our approach to prospecting and make it a meaningful use of both the customer's time and ours.

Effective Prospecting

Effective prospecting is different in that its goal is not to find new business as much as it is to anticipate it. And the beauty of this approach is that whether or not the business is found, this work is not a waste of time. This prospecting method occurs in three steps.

1. Conduct a simple analysis of one's territory and determine which accounts offer the greatest potential for sales revenue.

2. After that list is developed, designate which of these accounts currently use your product. Those that use your product should have files on them that tell, among other things, how many years they have had your product, and what is its typical lifecycle. In other words, if they've been using your product for four years, and its typical lifecycle is six years, then you need to start selling them on the benefits of upgrading to the newer model that you offer.

3. Develop this same information for all of the large accounts you call on who do not use your product. Those accounts that are nearing the end of their typical lifecycle are prospects.

Finally, once the largest accounts are mapped out, then some of the mid-sized accounts should be covered in the same way. But the smaller accounts do not justify the expenditure of a salesperson's most precious commodity: time.

Visiting Competitive Accounts

You've compiled a list of large accounts that are nearing the end of a normal product lifecycle and now it is time to visit them to accomplish the following:

1. Shape their perception of you.

2. Develop an understanding of their needs, hopes, fears, etc.

3. Shape their perception of your product and its differences.

The salesperson needs to establish the mindset that he is a non-threatening asset available to the customer at any time. The following approach has worked:

> **Salesperson:** Hi decision maker, your current system is about eight years old and is probably approaching the end of its lifecycle. Are you considering replacing it?
>
> **Customer:** No, not at this time.
>
> **Salesperson:** Fair enough. Our customers tell us one of the greatest things about our system is the way it took care of [fill in the blank with a known weakness of the competitive system they are using].
>
> But more importantly, they like the way we customized our product to help them reach their goals. Some of their goals were reducing turnover and improving efficiency. Can I ask you what some of your highest priority goals are?
>
> **Customer:** Reducing turnover is one of them.
>
> **Salesperson:** Great. I am going to send you some information that shows how our system will help you achieve this goal. And I'll give you the names and numbers of some of the customers who used our product to achieve this goal. You should give them a call. They'd be happy to hear from you.

In the above example, the salesperson immediately touched upon a known area of discomfort caused by the existing system. He showed how his system solved this problem and then, by asking a single, powerful question, began changing the customer's perception of him as a salesperson. How much more likely will this customer consider replacing their old system when they realize one of their personal goals can be reached by buying it? To be first is to finish first, and cause buying decisions.

Improving the Odds

The best way to improve one's odds for prospecting success is to network your way into an account. If the primary decision maker is called or emailed by someone he knows and trusts, and is told he needs to make time for you because you solved his problems with your product, then get ready for a fun sales call.

It can take a lot of work to keep a customer satisfied, and most customers know and appreciate this fact. If you have taken the time to service your customers, then they will likely help you, because you have helped them. Take advantage of this. Customers may have an instinctive distrust of salespeople they do not know, but this is diminished, or is completely erased, when they receive a call from a trusted friend who sings your praises.

The Treasure Map

Before the plans were made, or before he knew of them, General George S. Patton, by looking at a map, could see how the U.S. Army would advance across Europe. It was determined by where the roads led as much as anything else. Roads were needed to supply the massive army, and speed up the advance of infantry, tanks and artillery, so the advance would necessarily follow the roads. Like a general before a battle we need to study maps of our territory and, if they don't exist, create them.

Prospecting is developing a map of future opportunities. It shows you where you need to go to increase the odds of your success. These odds are improved by finding an opportunity before anyone else does and, therefore, prospecting needs to be a high priority for every salesperson.

Retention and Dominance

Whoever develops this map, it needs to become and remain the possession of the company who employed this salesperson. Can you imagine a company paying for a geological survey and allowing the surveyor to leave with his work even after he was paid in full?

Many software packages allow companies to develop what amounts to a treasure map. Their salespeople are supposed to input information on decision makers, their needs, wants, fears, names of their children, birthdays, etc. Every company engaging in complex sales should have such a system. Then, when a decision maker moves to another location, you may be the only company who possesses a file of valuable information on this person. Imagine your salesperson welcoming a relocated VP with a note that says:

> Hi Pat, your former salesperson, Chris, wanted to make sure I not only welcomed you and congratulated you on your recent move, but also promise to take excellent care of you. To fulfill my promise I wanted to schedule a brief meeting with you after you've had a chance to settle in.
>
> Chris told me you like Italian restaurants, and I know of a nice one not too far from your office. Once you get some spare time, perhaps we could meet for lunch?

Does this salesperson have an advantage over everyone who cannot act in like fashion? Also, not only is a company archiving valuable information, they are providing the salesperson who accumulated this data a powerful reason to stay on board. To uncover this information is hard work, and the salesperson who accomplishes this will want to enjoy the fruit of their labor. If they quit and join another company, then all of their hard work benefits someone else.

Information is not power, nor is knowledge. Anyone can possess all of this information about a customer and still be outsold by the person who possesses less information, but understands how to use it. But when you combine this information with the causes of the buying decision you will help to make your company dominant in its industry. I've seen it happen, and it is a great feeling to be on the winning side of this equation.

The Dangers of Presenting Second, or Last

The presentation order is another area where being first is best. I remember a customer, who favored us, asking me if I wanted to present last. This is the preferred slot of most salespeople.

I said, "Thank you for the offer; but if it's possible, may I be the first to present?"

She said, "Sure. But I thought you would want to be last."

"No," I replied, "first is great."

To Be First Is...

By being first I was able to tell customers what to fear and what to hope for. I could form a product-mindset based on our competitive advantages. And I could give them ideas about what to check out in the competitive systems that were being presented after me, and no one could do that to me.

I gave a presentation to a large hospital on the west coast and suggested the customers have the competitors, who followed me, shut their system down and then boot them back up. I did it to our system and showed how the downtime was minimal, but I knew my competitors would need almost the full hour to reboot their system. The customer complied. Afterwards, when a competitive salesperson left the room and his boss asked him how it went, he replied, "You know, I was dancing." I bet he was, from one land mine to another. They lost the sale and we won it.

If I am a consultant to the customer, I need to reveal the competitive system's shortcomings. Did they want a balky, unreliable system? They did not. Were they happy someone revealed to them just how balky and unreliable the expensive, competitive systems were? They were delighted, because it helped them steer clear of a bad buying decision. Besides, if a product has a known flaw, and the company fails to fix it, or the sales and marketing group fails to address it in a satisfactory way, then that company and salesperson do not deserve the vote of confidence represented by a customer's purchase order.

Before I left, one of the decision makers came out of the presentation room and said to me, "We did what you said. We asked them to shut down their system. They clearly did not want to do this, but they eventually did."

"How did that work out for them?" I asked.

"Not well."

Why would a customer volunteer this information to a salesperson during a competitive bid situation? I can only guess, but I believe it was because they were grateful that I helped differentiate our product from everyone else's.

We've covered the primacy effect, going first, but isn't there also a recency effect associated with going last?

Primacy or Recency Effect?

There is both a primacy effect and a recency effect, according to psychological studies. In other words, sometimes it is better to present first and other times it is better to go last. The recency effect—going last—is influential in those situations where several presentations are made and a decision is immediately made at the end of the presentations. The primacy effect, however, is influential when there is a delay between the presentations and the decision.[10]

In my experience, most of our complex sales had a considerable delay between the presentations and the decision to buy, so this made going first preferable. But even if the decision was made immediately after the last presentation, I would still prefer to go first, because I would be able to create a mindset that favored my product. This mindset tended to resist change and shape the customer's perceptions about the competitor's product in an unfavorable way. Also, I was able to plant land mines for those who followed me, and this more than offset the bias caused by the recency effect and presenting last.

Not First, or Last, but Uninvited

At the beginning of my career with Small Midwestern, a large, respected hospital network on the west coast issued a Request For Information to all of our competitors. We weren't even included on this initial list. I thought, "Yikes! We aren't even being invited to the dance." Instead of being first or second to an opportunity we were in the depressing category of "irrelevant and ignored."

By using differentiation we were not only able to muscle our way onto the list of competitors, we were able to win this order to install systems in two hospitals for around $5 million. Had we not used differentiation we probably would not have been allowed to compete.

Differentiation probably takes more advantage of the emotional causes of the buying decision than any other sales technique. This

---

[10] Plous, p. 45.

To Be First Is…

may account for its impact. If you are not using this skill, then I would encourage you to add it to your repertoire.

It's time to introduce you to what is the most powerful sales tool the salesperson can directly employ.

Part Two:

Powerful Presentations

6: Differentiation Is Powerful

The Stacked Deck

Sometimes you are dealt a hand that seems like it came from a stacked deck. Your sales situation seems impossible, but you have to move forward. And if you are unable to differentiate, then you might as well call in sick.

This true story involves a company we'll call Acme, which was much larger than its competitor, Small Midwestern, for whom I worked. Acme was also widely admired across the country. Meanwhile, Small Midwestern was scarcely known to the primary decision makers—in this instance, high-ranking nurses.

At the large hospital where this scene was staged, Acme had a particularly powerful advantage. The nurses loved them. Additionally, they hated Small Midwestern's Region Manager and barred him from entering their hospital.

The one advantage Small Midwestern had was being on a national buying agreement while Acme was not. These agreements are frequently disregarded. They don't have much in the way of teeth to enforce them. But the hospital's administration refused to buy the Acme product until these nurses listened to a presentation from Small Midwestern.

Since Small Midwestern's Region Manager was banned from the account, the administrator called our corporate office and asked me to fly down to present to this group. He gave me the background and I thought, "Oh joy. I am being sent to a hostile crowd who is forced to listen to me. This will be interesting."

The Power of the Emotional Approach

After being introduced by the same administrator who was forcing them to attend my presentation, I opened my mouth to speak. That was the signal for the nurses to launch their ambush. For several minutes the head nurse unleashed an ear-blistering screed covering Small Midwestern's sins, mortal and venial, sins of omission and commission, and when she finished she just stared at me. I got the uneasy sense that she was visually checking my vitals to see if I could still fog a mirror and continue.

I don't think she expected what happened next. I smiled like I was the happiest person in the world to be there, and then responded, "I want to thank you for bringing up all of these issues. They're important. Every one of them will be addressed."

After I addressed them I forged ahead and said, "And now I would like to go over the goals of this presentation." I told them how I was going to cover some of the many areas that were important to them, and then said something that is critical to the differentiation process:

> Ultimately, when you make a decision it will be based on the differences between the two systems. They both do very different things. Since this is our first time together, I need to tell you how our product is different from our competitors so that you can make an informed decision. These differences are significant and important. They are directly tied to what each system can and can't do.
>
> My statements will be fact based. I am not interested in slamming my competitor because they are a phenomenal company with phenomenal salespeople. And to make sure it is fact based I would ask you a favor: if at any time you know I am wrong on a point, or even if you think I am, please interrupt me and let me know.

The reason why I say this is because our marketing department does a great job of gathering information about our competitors, but we do not have a direct line of communication with our competitors and you do. They may have changed their product and we might not know about it yet. So, let me know if I am off base on something. Okay? Let's get started.

We return to the subject of mindsets. They form quickly, resist change and assimilate new information to fit the mindset's image. I mention this because my introduction was designed to form a mindset that allowed me to speak about the competition without fear of offending. I was creating an image of myself as the honest broker of objective information. It was not a false image, because I made sure that everything I said was correct. Or, if I happened to be misinformed, I invited correction from anyone who might be better informed.

I followed this by introducing the buyers to our position in the market, some of the great solutions we offered, and then began to attack the competitor where they were weak. They offered a less robust communication package and a large Emergency Department needed a platform that would support communications between caregivers, patients, physicians and other departments like the pharmacy. I pointed out how we had dozens of references proving we could do what I believed they wanted in this area, and how our competitors, to our knowledge, had none. I asked them to please provide me with a single reference the competitor offered them so that we could check it out and change our story if need be. There was no reference. Our competitor could not do what we could and this point struck a nerve.

The decision makers were silent and seething, but their staff began to spontaneously interject comments like, "We've got to have that capability!" "Why are we even getting a new system if it can't do that?" More eruptions in our favor began to occur. The tide was turning. Now the decision makers would have to decide for a product not favored by their own staff and the administration, or decide for us. We learned within days that we closed the sale.

The Causes of Sales Success

Let's review how unlikely it was for me to cause this customer's favorable buying decision:

1. The customer loved the competitor's company, product and representative.

2. The customer hated us and I got to experience a concentrated dose of this.

3. Our customer was forced by the administration to listen to my presentation. This was not the way to generate positive feelings or perceptions of me, my product or my company.

4. I was given one shot to reverse their decision and that shot was about one hour in duration.

5. From both an emotional and a rational outlook I appeared to be a dog's breakfast served to a pampered pooch.

How could this system, or any other, deliver a winning hand when the deck was stacked against me?

Simple. If you know what causes sales to close, and you apply this knowledge with focus and skill, then even stacked decks can be reshuffled. Emotions cause the buying decision, and I turned to what may be the most powerful emotion in the salesperson's tool kit: fear.

Fear

Fear is one of the most powerful emotions there is in a selling situation. It is not always appropriate, but it can have a devastating impact on a competitor no matter how favored they are. The best way to generate the type of fear that favorably influences a buying decision is through differentiation. This technique shows how your product does something that a competitor's cannot. It then ties this competitive shortcoming to problems that generate strong emotions. Soon the customer begins to fear buying a product that is inadequate.

Differentiation won the sale in many difficult selling situations, and not just this one. It helped to sell our system to customers who were vocally opposing us up until the moment our final presentation began. One of the more memorable occasions now follows. At every step, this customer's irrational bias was on full display.

"You Know What I Think of Your Stuff."

We were trying to break into a city that was one of our top competitor's strongholds. They had a salesperson who had strong relationships with powerful decision makers throughout this city's largest accounts. We found out about an opportunity at one of them, and my Region Manager went to visit it with our distributor. After this meeting, my Region Manager wrote the following in his call report (all of the names have been changed):

> Harriet [the primary decision maker] arrived 20 minutes late and announced she didn't know why she was even there. ...Harriet said she needed the system to have ease of connection and interact well with [one of our competitor's other products].

This competitor's salespeople routinely planted this objection. It was something our product could not do. The story continued to unfold in his call report:

> While there was a conversation between me and another, Harriet leaned over to Jill [the distributor salesperson] and told her "I've met with you several times and you know what I think of your stuff." Interesting comment considering Jill is new to [our distributor] and has never been at [this hospital] before.

> Our chances at winning this project are marginal but the best they have ever been or ever will be.

Marginal chances are what differentiation makes a living off of. During the needs analysis phase that followed, the Region Manager also noted:

> Harriet is a bit of a loose cannon. She gets so caught up into trying to [support] her need to have [our competitor's product that] she can become illogical in her arguments. She

doesn't seem to really know [their] system so [she] just locks onto the few key features she seems coached [on]….

Illogical? Did someone say the decision is emotional in nature and not rational?

Again, it is counter-intuitive to enter a situation like this and think, "Let's paint our competitor, who is loved, in a bad light," but it is your only option. After all, how can a reasoned argument compete against the power of an emotional attachment? Try to reason someone out of being in love. It doesn't work, because reason is not strong enough to sever these emotional bonds. The only thing that has a chance of succeeding is to introduce a more powerful emotion to replace, or overpower, the existing one and that is what differentiation does. It introduces the emotion of fear, the dread of making a bad decision that will haunt the decision maker for as long as she works at that location.

Harriet was now at our corporate headquarters and I was slated to present first. Moments before I spoke Harriet said, "I think your reliability is a problem."

Reliability was one of our product's greatest strengths, and our company had traditionally focused on this benefit. Therefore, Harriet was attempting to remove what she believed to be our primary benefit seconds before I started to present.

She continued, "I pray your [older generation system] dies so we are forced to get rid of it. As it is, it never dies and I'm stuck with this system that can't do what I want or need."

I thought, "This ought to be fun. Here we go." And it was fun. Harriet kicked and screamed the entire time en route to issuing us a purchase order.

Step 1: Securing the Right to Differentiate

Prior to differentiating, I sell the customer on the need to make a product comparison, and I do this whether the crowd is friendly or hostile—we can never be 100% certain what their attitude is.

Differentiation Is Powerful

I usually start by asking them, "Can you tell me the differences between the products?" This question works for me no matter how they answer it. Suppose they say, "No." I then respond, "If you don't know the differences between the competitive systems at the end of this evaluation, then you might as well flip a coin, because until you know their differences they will appear to be the same. We find that our customers appreciate being told the differences, because it helps them make an informed decision at the end of this process."

In the rare cases when the customer responds *yes, we know some of the differences*, I then ask, "And what are they?" In almost every case I have found them to be differences favoring the competitive product, which leads me to reply, "I can tell by the nature of these differences that our competitor has been doing his job and that is *telling you how our products are different*. To make an informed decision you need to know these differences, so I will continue the process he began, and tell you about some of the important differences you failed to mention."

If they were ever to mention differences that favored us, I would congratulate them for knowing some and ask if they knew any others. Once they exhausted their list, I would reply:

> Excellent! You've almost done my job for me. When we pose this same question to most of our other customers we find they cannot give us a single difference, and you've named three. Now I am happy to tell you there are several other powerful and important solutions our product offers that the competitive products do not. I think you will find they make our system even more unique and valuable.

In the story of the stacked deck, and in the illustration just given, I've shown ways to secure the right to differentiate, but there are other ways to do this. For example, I might illustrate the evaluation process, and the problems it causes:

> We have found that after a customer has listened to four or five of these presentations all of the facts start to become a blur. They are now faced with making a very expensive decision, and they are not sure which system does what. What they tell us helps them is for us to spell out the

differences as clearly as possible, so that they can then research these areas on their own; so that is what I am going to be doing in my presentation.

This is quickly followed by one of the most important parts of the exercise.

Step 2: Develop the Mindset

I stumbled upon this idea of mindsets while reading a CIA manual found online. What struck me about this psychological mechanism was its almost irresistible power. Even though the CIA's analysts are aware of this tendency of the mind, they still fall into this mental trap of developing mindsets that will influence their evaluation of intelligence.[11] Therefore, knowledge of this process does not prevent it from still working in many cases, if not most. These same limitations affect everyone, including our customers.

Creating this differentiation-mindset never involves saying something like, "I am an honest broker of objective information." Instead, we create this mindset by saying things that suggest we are such a person. All of our words and actions that follow will then reinforce this image.

At the beginning of my presentations I would say something like:

> In this comparison I will be presenting the facts as objectively as possible. [True.] This information is based on the latest marketing research that we have [True.] and if you know or believe anything I say to be untrue, then please interrupt me and let's discuss it. The reason I ask you to do this is because you have an advantage that I don't. Our competitor will tell you the latest and greatest developments

---

[11] Heuer, p. 1. The book begins with this summary statement introducing *Chapter One, Thinking About Thinking*: "Of the diverse problems that impede accurate intelligence analysis, those inherent in human mental processes are surely among the most important and most difficult to deal with. Intelligence analysis is fundamentally a mental process, but understanding this process is hindered by the lack of conscious awareness of the workings of our own minds."

about his product, but he will not tell me, so some of what I tell you may have changed without our being aware of it.

When you tell the customer about a difference between the two products you must always be honest and accurate. Always. And you really do want to know if you have misstated something, because if you have, and you continue to do so in other presentations, it might diminish your presentation's effectiveness.

Step 3: The Differentiation Presentation

To avoid offending, or the appearance of bashing, it is important to follow these rules during a presentation:

1. Tone is all-important. When differentiating I adopt an almost clinically dispassionate voice, because I know an emotional tone will evoke an emotional response. If I sneeringly say, "Their product can become unstable when it tries to handle heavy data traffic, and I will tell you why," then the audience will immediately think I am bashing the competitor. If I say the exact same words in a dispassionate voice, they are not offended at all. So, do not use an emotional tone when making these product comparisons.

2. Never overstate the facts. Differentiation does not go for the carotid-artery to inflict a quick kill. It is more like inflicting the death of a thousand cuts. In effective differentiation no one point is sufficient to win the day when up against a favored competitor, but after inflicting numerous wounds the competitor slowly begins to stumble and fall. Here is an example of what I mean by understating the facts. Suppose a competitor is misleadingly telling a customer that it can make its product integrate with another important system, but there is no evidence that it can and plenty of evidence that it cannot. I never say, "Their system cannot do this," even if I believe this to be true. This sort of direct language is too confrontational. Instead I say, "I know of no place in the country where this integration has been made to work, and if you have a specific reference site where you have <u>seen</u> this integration work, then please let me know so that I can

change what I say in my presentations." Does this not accomplish the same thing as the blunter statement? No, it accomplishes much more. The blunt statement may have the customer silently thinking, "But our rep told us it works in a business on the east coast. This guy doesn't know what he's talking about." The softer statement will have them wondering, "I haven't actually seen it work. Did they not give us references on this?"

3. Never attack the competitor's salesperson even when he or she is guilty of telling the most outrageous lies. To do so would be to invite a decision maker to defend them since they are absent and cannot defend themselves. When confronted with an obvious lie I ask, "May I ask where you heard this?" If they tell me, "From your competitor." I reply, "The exact opposite is the case, and this fact has been known for several years throughout our industry, so I am very surprised he does not know about this." The customer can draw their own conclusions and it just could be this salesperson is new, or was told the wrong information from their marketing department. I was a salesperson once and have been fed misinformation, so I know it happens.

4. Rehearse extensively prior to differentiating in front of a hostile audience. As you are gently undermining the position of their friend—your competitor—they will be watching you like a hawk. Can you look them in the eye and speak with a steady, authoritative tone, or does your voice crack with nervousness? The style of your presentation is often more important than its substance.

5. Be as factually accurate as possible. If you make more than one mistake, the audience will begin to think, "Does this guy know what he is talking about?" For ethical and practical reasons, be accurate and honest.

Accused of Bashing

A salesperson made a clumsy stab at differentiation and a decision influencer, Barbara, said in a withering tone, "Listen here. You may

Differentiation Is Powerful

get mileage out of bashing the competition elsewhere, but you will not get anywhere with me. Is that understood?" She meekly said, "Yes," and then waited an eternity for that moment to pass.

A week later Barbara was coming to see a second presentation at the distributor's showroom. I was scheduled to present. The question was, "Should I differentiate?"

If this important decision influencer was in the audience I thought it would be a bad idea to differentiate, because she might now have a mindset that we are a company of bashers. To differentiate might reinforce this mindset and generate negative emotions. So, we removed all differentiating slides, stories, etc., from the presentation.

Then, shortly before the customer group arrived, I found out Barbara was not going to attend this presentation. I then quickly changed my presentation back to its original, differentiating format, because I felt differentiation offered us the best chance for success. This was a three-hospital system in the backyard of an entrenched competitor and winning this account would not be easy. My presentation with all of its differentiating slides was on the screen awaiting the arrival of our guests when Barbara walked through the door with the rest of the group.

What was I to do? They were in the room where the presentation was being given. I could not change it in front of them. Therefore, I differentiated our product, followed the principles outlined in this chapter and this, along with the efforts of others, secured the job. I was not accused of bashing.

Here is the point. It appears that you can effectively differentiate in all situations, and since it is so powerful, why wouldn't you? Our customer had an emotional bond with our competitor that was strengthened by years of business dealings. Would a logical argument sever this strong tie? No. What was required was a stronger emotion, and that emotion was fear.

Final note on this story: Why did the salesperson's differentiation attempt fail while mine succeeded? Two things likely happened. First, she probably skipped the important preliminary step of creating a mindset wherein she became the honest broker of objective information. Second, she likely overplayed her hand and differentiated too strongly. One does not go for the jugular with this technique. Also, one approaches differentiation humbly, for as soon as we appear arrogant in our presentation we are likely to overreach and fall.

It could also be that differentiation is a difficult skill for many to master. If you are interested in having your salesforce trained in this technique, then please send a note to: tom@essentialgrowthsolutions.com.

Differentiation Builds Trust

To differentiate is to act like a consultant. To appear to be a consultant generates the emotion of trust. Yes, mentioning the competitor actually fosters a stronger relationship.

We once had a customer who came to our office favoring a competitor, having bought their expensive system before. As I went into the differentiation, she began to see why this competitive product she was using was never able to do some of the things she had always wanted it to do. Also, the competitor never gave her a satisfactory answer about its limitations. She then looked at me and asked, "Why haven't they fixed this?"

Now at this point the competitor is lying in front of me with their jugular exposed. The customer obviously respects my forthrightness and my desire to be accurate and honest in this presentation. Based on this perception of me she has new expectations normally not associated with salespeople. She turns to me as if I were a paid consultant who was hired to help her make a decision. If you find yourself in this position be very careful.

First, you have gained the customer's trust, and this precious gift needs to be respected and nurtured. So now is not the time to rip your competitor to shreds no matter how abusive they are, or may have been in the past. For this reason I responded, "I have no idea why they haven't fixed this. To offer an explanation would be pure speculation on my part."

To which she replied, "Speculate, please."

I then offered her my honest opinion of possible reasons why they had not fixed one of their system's biggest shortcomings, and she became our customer. What is remarkable is the way my product comparison resulted in her treating me as if I was a paid consultant working for her. Differentiation, when performed well, builds trust, and building trust is one of our primary goals.

Not a Silver Bullet

Differentiation is undeniably powerful, but it is often not sufficient to win the sale by itself. It is a great momentum changer, but it does not always close the sale. For example, what if the points you are making during a differentiation presentation fail to inspire fear? What if the customer's response is, "Their product can't do that? Interesting, but not critical."

If your differentiation fails to hit the mark, the other parts of your presentation had better work. To become a better presenter is of critical importance when it comes to causing buying decisions. Few things generate powerful emotions more effectively than our words, and the presentation is when the customer hears us speak. One of the ways we make our words more powerful is by creating and delivering stories. If you use them, and your competition does not, it is another way of separating yourself from the pack.

7: Powerful Stories

Don Hewitt, the man who created the long running hit TV program, *60 Minutes*, said he followed this simple formula: "It's four little words. Tell me a story."[12] What made *60 Minutes* such a great success was not its reporting of the news, but the way it turned news into stories with drama, heightened conflict and pace.

A good story is captivating, and this explains part of a story's power. In an age of constant distraction—think, texting while driving—stories hold a person's attention. This is critical, because if the customer ain't listening, you ain't selling. But the most remarkable thing about stories is the way they are memorable. Sometimes I would start a training class with a story on Monday, then check to see if the class remembered it on Friday, and they did. As the great English writer, Rudyard Kipling, once wrote, "If history were taught in the form of stories, it would never be forgotten."

Presentations benefit immensely from stories. The customer's mind that often wanders during a presentation becomes attentive once a good story hooks them, because they want to find out how this story ends. Then, after all of the data dumped upon them by your competitors is quickly forgotten, your story that vividly described a problem they are experiencing, and how it was solved, lingers on in their mind.

---

[12] This quotation can be found on the web at the following address: http://www.cbsnews.com/8301-18560_162-5257828.html

So how do you construct a story that is tight, powerful, and memorable? What follows is a summary of the workshop that showed many students how it is done.

Workshop

Before arriving at the training class, the students were assigned the following task. Write a story that illustrates a solution our product, or your distributorship, provides the customer. It can be no longer than two minutes and it must follow this form:

Step one: hook the audience with a problematic situation.

Step two: detail the actions taken to resolve this situation.

Step three: paint a picture of the satisfying payoff.

It sounds simple, doesn't it? It is, but simplicity is rarely easy. Reducing something to its simplest elements can take hours of thought and effort. Though the task we gave them seemed easy, they struggled with it. Their initial stories were all in need of work. Yet they kept at it, because after they heard a good story they realized just how powerful a story could be. After extensive editing almost everyone had a powerful story to tell.

An Example of a Story that Sells

The following story shows how a distributor could highlight their service credentials in a memorable way. Imagine a salesperson standing in front of customers and providing the following introduction:

> One thing our customers like the most about our company is its unparalleled commitment to service. I think this is best illustrated by an event that occurred last year.

The Story Begins With a Situation

> One of our hospitals was crippled by a massive lightning strike that took out most of their electronic systems. It happened on Christmas Eve and our technicians were on vacation.

The situation introduces a problem that creates tension. It hooks the audience who wants to know, "What happens next?" This is a particularly powerful hook for hospital employees; for when a home loses power, then food spoils and people may suffer from the heat or cold. But when a hospital loses power from a lightning strike it is a potential life and death situation, because equipment that is keeping people alive—ventilators, etc.—may have been damaged by the power surge.

The Story Continues With the Actions Taken

> But we always have a technician on call every hour of every day. Over the phone, he got a sense of the magnitude of the problem and called another tech, who was also on vacation, to help.
>
> Before they left for the hospital, they increased the number of parts they normally carried in their trucks. They needed the extra parts.
>
> Within two hours we had two technicians on site testing the system to determine the extent of the damage.

An Analysis of the "Actions Taken" Section

The goal of the story is to present this distributorship as a superlative service organization that is dedicated to the customer. The details that support this goal are presented in the "Actions Taken" segment.

The *Actions Taken* section began with:

> But we always have a technician on call every hour of every day.

This detail shows the distributor's dedication to the customer's needs at all times. The customer has likely suffered from a slow response, or even unresponsiveness, from a vendor. In most instances this caused inconvenience. In the instance of this lightning strike, the negative impact of a delay would have been much greater.

The story continued:

Powerful Stories

> Over the phone, he got a sense of the magnitude of the problem and called another tech, who was also on vacation, to help.

This detail shows how the culture of the organization is one wherein the customer comes first. The tech calls to bother another person. Now two families are having their Christmas holiday disturbed to take care of a customer. The customer may have had to sacrifice a holiday with their family in the past, and will then feel kinship with a company that does what it takes to get their job done.

> Before they left for the hospital, they increased the number of parts they normally carried in their trucks.

The distributor shows how their expertise led them to prepare for the worst. This sped up the repair process.

> They needed the extra parts.

This detail serves to engage the audience. It illustrates the magnitude of their challenge and makes the pay-off at the end of the story even more impressive.

> Within two hours we had two technicians on site testing the system to determine the extent of the damage.

The service is prompt even under extreme conditions.

Finally, note how the actions need to be definite and not fuzzy. Details are critical, but they must support the goal of the story. The salesperson now concludes his story with the results of their actions.

The Story Concludes With the Results, or Pay-off

> In less than eight hours all of the problems were identified, compromised parts were replaced, and the database was uploaded. This hospital was fully functional after a catastrophic failure on Christmas Eve eight hours after it occurred. All of their other electrical systems were down for much longer. They are still talking about that one.

The pay-off should be:

- To the point.

- Demonstrate the delivery of a benefit or solution to the customer that is highly valued.

- If it can differentiate you from your competitors, or even others who service your customer in different capacities, then be sure to include that detail. In the above example the salesperson includes the telling detail, "All of their other electrical systems were down for much longer." In other words, our service far-outshined everyone else's.

In less than one minute a salesperson delivered a large quantity of information praising his company's service capability in a way that did not sound like a sales pitch. It is memorable, engaging, entertaining and not what most customers are used to hearing.

Compare the efficacy of the above story to this wordy data-dump, complete with all of the extraneous verbiage that typically clutters the unrehearsed sales pitch:

> We are the best of the best when it comes to service. Our service is 24-7-365. Like I said, the best. We have three fully stocked trucks available, and we've never needed more than these three trucks to be on site anywhere in our territory in one hour or less. We used to have two trucks, but we are excited about the way three trucks give us more flexibility, and improve our response times. Our technicians are all factory trained in every system they work on. They've received customer service training. They have a combined tenure of 45 years with our company. It is highly likely they know your hospital's technical staff on a first-name basis. This staff is available to you for the first year at no additional charge. They've won awards from the manufacturers they represent in nine of the last ten years.

Blah, blah, blah, blah.

Sorry. If you didn't make it through the above paragraph, I understand, because a customer would also mentally bail on a data dump. The mind just cannot absorb the bits of data fast enough, determine their value, and keep pace with the continuing cascade of facts.

Using Several Stories In a Presentation

If the customer ain't listening, you ain't selling. Therefore, it is critical to keep the customer's mind engaged in your presentation. Even when you successfully illustrate solutions for your customer in a way that is both interesting and easy to digest, eventually they will need to come up for air. Therefore, I try to include a story in a presentation every seven to eight minutes. That means seven to eight stories per hour of presenting. The number of stories, of course, can be less, but they should not be more.

A key determinant of how many stories you will ultimately use is both their power and their applicability. Do they capture the customer's attention and imagination? Do they deliver the emotional goods in a memorable fashion? Do they address a customer's problems and needs? If they meet these criteria, then why wouldn't you want to use such a story?

I still remember stories I heard over forty years ago, and this is perhaps the most important thing about a story: If it touches an emotional chord, it can stay with the customer for weeks or months. Does this give you an advantage?

Even when the customer cannot immediately recall your story due to the way their busy day distracts them and befogs their mind, it can still resurface days or weeks later when it is time to make a decision. As they review your promotional/bid literature—where you make sure the essence of your stories appear—a case study, or a few sentences can immediately bring your stories to mind. It will also bring up a favorable memory of you, and how your presentation was the only one that did not make them feel like they were being subjected to the sales version of the Chinese Water Torture: data, data, data, data, drip, drip, drip, drip.

Making Your Story Better

The first draft of a story is rarely any good; so if your story is awful do not despair. Great stories are typically ones that go through many rewrites. Here are some guidelines to follow to make your story better.

The Topic Must Be Interesting and Relevant

The first step is picking a great topic, and these guidelines may help you locate several:

1. Go down a list of satisfied customers and find out what makes them satisfied. The more emotional their response the greater the likelihood that this feedback contains the kernel of a great story.

2. If a customer, unsolicited, ever contacted you to tell you how great your product performed, then a story topic is likely buried in this response.

3. Any example of your product solving a vexing problem for a customer has great potential.

4. Are there any examples of your product doing something that no other product can, and does this deliver tremendous value to the customer? Then a story can likely be found in what your product does.

5. Here is a simple rule: if you don't have a hook, you don't have a story.

Assemble the Materials

After you pick a topic, you need to separate the material into three baskets. One will cover the problem a customer faced that needed solving. The more dramatic you can truthfully make it, the better. The second basket covers the actions taken. Here you want to collect as many concrete actions as possible. You will sort through these actions during the rewrite and discard the weaker ones. Finally, you need to have a satisfying pay-off that occurred as a direct result of the actions taken. This pay-off is the third basket.

The three parts of the story have different objectives so it helps to tackle the story section by section, rather than trying to write it all at once.

Write Your Story and Begin Editing

When you've assembled your three baskets, write each section of your story. When you've finished writing, go back and do your best to cut out half of the words. While you edit your material, your guidelines are: If it can be cut, cut it. If it does not advance the story toward the pay-off, cut it. If it can be expressed more concisely, then make it more concise.

To illustrate the editing process I will give you an example of a story taken from a workshop I conducted on interviewing. The workshop used the ideas of this book to arm the job-search candidate with skills that helped separate them from the pack of competitors who were vying for the same job. Among the skills they were taught was how to create and utilize stories in both their interview and on their resume.

One of the workshop attendees was a delightful, middle-aged woman. She developed this story as a way of convincing an interviewer that she could handle pressure situations. Names, places and facts are changed from her original version. *Much of her text has a line running through it.* That is because most of what she wrote was deleted. Her struggles with the story form are similar to those of salespeople and illustrate common challenges posed by this medium.

> I was working for XYZ Travel ~~in Tucson, Oklahoma for John Smith, a really~~ tough boss ~~who either loved you or hated you. If he came to hate you, you didn't work there anymore and dared not darken his door again. If he came to love you, he drove you to be the best you could be and I learned a lot on that job. The only reason I left was to be a partner in an agency of my own.~~

Too many words, too many meaningless details, too conversational a tone…there was not a lot of salvageable material in this first paragraph. However, where she worked is part of the story she is trying to tell. Conflict makes a story dramatic and interesting, so this "tough boss" detail is kept; but the rest of the details fail to advance the story. Also, where is the hook?

The Causes of Sales Success

> ~~One day Dr. Stan Jones paid us a visit.~~ He pioneered a medical procedure at a prestigious hospital. ~~Being used to a high caliber, demanding clientele because I handled most of John's personal friends and associates, Dr. Jones won the dubious honor of being the~~ most taxing traveler ~~I had ever encountered in fifteen years of experience in the travel industry.~~

The first sentence of the above paragraph was unnecessary. But the fact that this doctor was among the best in his profession was a good detail, as was his being difficult. Both points advance the story toward its goal of showing how she could handle pressure. The rest of the paragraph was pointless piffle.

> ~~He had $XX, XXX to take~~ a trip around the world with his companion, wanted to be gone two months and was leaving in two weeks. ~~All customized travel with a few "canned" excursions thrown in meaning I didn't have to call Cairo and find a boat to rent along the Nile. But there was no such thing as e-mail or fax machines in the mid-eighties. Everything was done by telephone. Telex, or snail mail, and an airline computer or typewriter.~~

A concise expression of the task she faced was all that was needed in this wordy paragraph. The details about the days before email, etc., only served to date her, so it was deleted. The paragraph below, that ends her situation, was why they invented delete keys. I share it to show how ruthlessly you must edit your stories.

> ~~John had the habit of promising everything to clients and then handing it over to me saying, "Make it happen!" Plus, it went without saying to be efficient and make money while I was at it. John told Dr. Jones that I was his best agent and Dr. Jones told John, if I couldn't do it, I wasn't worth my salt… I am a people person but goal oriented by challenge.~~

Analysis and the Final Product

I include this example because it shows how good stories can emerge from awful first drafts. This bad first draft demonstrates several of the problems people experience when they attempt to develop their own stories. Most salespeople struggle with getting to the point and sticking to it. Like the above person, they like to chatter. Delete all chatter.

Since this is the first stage of the story, I need to see a hook, and this stage did not have one. What is amazing is her story had a great hook that was buried in the middle of the *Actions Taken* stage. After working with her, we came up with an excellent story. I took the hook and moved it to the front of the story where it belongs.

Imagine her in front of an interviewer who asks, "How do you handle pressure situations?"

She responds, "I handle pressure situations extremely well. For example [her story follows]:

> While I was working for ABC Travel, Dr. Jones, a world famous doctor from the Mustard Clinic, wanted to take a two-month, multi-stop, around-the-world trip. And he wanted to leave in two weeks. This was a ridiculously short amount of time to coordinate the hundreds of details. What made this worse was the way both my boss, and this doctor, were demanding perfectionists. But there was a reason for the short notice. Dr. Jones was terminally ill. This would be his last trip.

It took around twenty seconds to turn a prosaic travel agent story into something gripping. It involves life and death. You want to know the end of the story.

Okay, I'll tell you. The doctor couldn't finish the entire trip. He became sick and returned to his prestigious hospital to be cared for. However, he was so impressed by the trip she planned, and what he had experienced, that he told everyone at the hospital about it, and this hospital became the travel agency's largest account.

Guidelines for Good Stories

1. Wordiness kills good stories. They turn a powerful tool into a dead weight that hurts your sales cause.

2. If you can't find a hook, then find another story. Once you find a hook, place it near the beginning of your story.

3. Actions taken are clear, not fuzzy. They advance the story toward the satisfying pay-off.

4. Details also advance the story. They are like flowers that make a garden beautiful. However, extraneous details add drag and not thrust, and the story burdened by them never takes off.

5. Each one of the most powerful emotional responses unearthed by the needs analysis should be addressed by a story if possible.

6. Stories should not be bunched together. One every 7-8 minutes is good so long as they are concise, entertaining, and pack an emotional punch.

7. Stories should never exceed two minutes. If it has to be two minutes, then place it near the beginning. Toward the end of a long presentation, shorter stories (about one minute) are better than longer ones (about two minutes).

8. If, during your rehearsing, you feel you have too many stories, then guess what? You have too many stories.

Conclusion

The power of stories comes from the way they can grab and hold a customer's attention, make your solutions memorable, and sell in a way that does not appear sales-y in the least. This is important, because people enjoy buying, but hate being sold.

In the next chapter we are going from the equivalent of blog posting—stories—to micro-blogging—a phrase or a sentence. When a memorable phrase or sentence is repeated it can generate great emotional power.

8: The Power of Words

Why are certain phrases and sentences so powerful they remain in our minds long after we first hear them? As the following shows, the style of the message that gives it emotional power:

> If the student doubts that style is something of a mystery, let him try rewriting a familiar sentence and see what happens. Any much-quoted sentence will do. Suppose we take "These are the times that try men's souls." Here are eight short, easy words, forming a simple declarative sentence. The sentence contains no flashy ingredients such as "Damn the torpedoes!" and the words, as you see, are ordinary. Yet in that arrangement, they have shown great durability; the sentence is almost into its third century. Now compare a few variations:
>
> Times like these try men's souls.
> How trying it is to live in these times.
> These are trying times for men's souls.
> Soulwise, these are trying times.[13]

The above variations repeat the substance of the original sentence, but fail to capture its style. This shows us how we are not concerned so much with coming up with a profound thought—substance—but

---

[13] William Strunk, Jr. & E. B. White, *The Elements of Style* (Boston: Allyn and Bacon, 1979), p. 67.

instead are trying to create a simple sentence or two that touches a customer where they emotionally live.

Quick aside: *The Elements of Style*, the source of the above quotation, should be owned and studied by every sales and marketing professional. There is perhaps no better primer on using words powerfully.

Politicians Understand the Power of Words

Some of the most sophisticated selling techniques are used during presidential campaigns. One insight we gain from studying politicians is how they believe in the power of words like few others. They literally spend millions of dollars to harness this power:

> In the post-Reagan era, most politicians have understood the importance of harnessing verbal and visual imagery in their effort to affect voter attitudes and opinions. Roughly one-half of President Clinton's annual $2 million polling budget is targeted toward communication, and it shows with every speech and public appearance. Bill Clinton "feels your pain" because he actually knows what your pain is.[14]

Presidential campaigns spend hundreds of thousands of dollars on focus groups to get feedback on which phrases or words hit home. Let's examine some of the successful campaigns and see if there is any linkage between a successfully worded message and victory.

Governor Jimmy Carter: "I'll never lie to you." If you google this phrase, up pops Mr. Carter. His idealism, expressed in this tag line from the campaign, was just what a Watergate-weary electorate wanted to hear.

Governor Ronald Reagan: "Are you any better off now than you were four years ago?" In this short sentence Mr. Reagan tapped into the fear of the electorate over another four years of President Jimmy Carter.

---

[14] Frank I. Luntz, *Voices of Victory, Part II, The Makings of a Good Focus Group* (quote found at http://www.pollingreport.com/focus.htm)

The Power of Words

In his second campaign President Ronald Reagan expressed the hope and optimism people were beginning to feel with the theme, "It's morning in America."

Vice President George H. W. Bush: "Read my lips, 'No new taxes.'" This message appealed to a country wanting to continue to enjoy the prosperity ushered in by the Reagan years. Then, when he flip-flopped on this campaign pledge, he lost his reelection battle. What was his tagline for his losing effort? It lacked any such coherent focus. At one point he jokingly said to reporters, "Read my hips," whatever that means.

Governor Bill Clinton: The successful Clinton campaign formulated this memorable message: "It's the economy, stupid." The American electorate agreed. This simple sentence let them know that Mr. Clinton was in touch with their pain and suffering. The "stupid" angle was a not-so-subtle way of repositioning President George H. W. Bush as being someone who just didn't get it.

Senator Bob Dole: When President Bill Clinton ran against Mr. Dole for his second term, Mr. Dole came up with this campaign vision: "I offer you a bridge to the past." Now that stirs the soul. To which Mr. Clinton replied, "I offer you a bridge to the future." That election was over before it began.

Governor George W. Bush & Vice President Al Gore: Mr. Bush portrayed his political philosophy as "compassionate conservatism." Mr. Gore defined his campaign by saying: "I am my own man." Neither candidate did a very good job of distilling their message to a single, defining phrase. The result was a virtual tie that was decided by the Supreme Court.

Senator Barack Obama: "Hope and change we can believe in." Even though he was a first term senator who had yet to finish his first term, America was war weary and change is what everyone wanted. As for Senator John McCain, who ran against Mr. Obama, he never seemed to get beyond his personal war-hero narrative. No memorable phrase expressed what his campaign represented.

The Emotional Message

Observe their phrases and their common emotional quality:

Trust: "I will never lie to you."

Fear of Carter's Return: "Are you any better off now than you were four years ago?"

Hope: "It's morning in America."

Money Is Emotion Quantified: "Read my lips. No new taxes."

Money Is Emotion Quantified: "It's the economy stupid."

Hope: "I offer you a bridge to the future."

Love: "I'm a compassionate conservative."

Hope and Trust: "Hope and change we can believe in."

From the ultimate selling effort, a presidential campaign, we can learn how powerful it is to distill your sales message to a simple phrase or sentence. It is memorable. But more than that, it reduces a complicated message to its single, most influential point, and that is what gives it its power.

How can we develop powerful phrases to assist our selling efforts? By following these steps.

Step One: Selecting a Few Words

The art of developing phrases begins with locating the words that generate an emotional response from your customer. It starts by asking, "What is it that your customer yearns for? And what is it about your product or service that people most value?"

Let's say you are in the service industry and your primary competitor focuses on delivering the lowest cost service. Your service, on the other hand, is more expensive because you deliver a better service experience to your customers. So how can you develop a phrase that persuades customers to spend more for your service?

What words come to mind that need to be a part of this campaign? From the functional arena you know that the word "service," or ones expressing what your industry does, can be used. Since your service delivers "customer satisfaction," and your customers value this enough to pay more for your service, then these words, or ones expressing this sentiment, could be a part of your phrase.

When you turn to an online thesaurus you find some synonyms of *satisfaction* are: Fulfillment, contentment, happiness, and so on. These words become possibilities for your phrase.

Finally, you turn to your satisfied customers and ask them why they are so happy with your service. Perhaps something they say will provide you with a new expression about why you are able to charge more and still compete effectively.

Once you have these words, then the phrase or sentence can be developed.

Step Two: Turning Words Into Phrases

Phrases will start to form as you mull over these words and ideas. Again, the first phrases may be truly awful, but we are not looking for the first swipe to hit a home run. It is usually in the editing process that these rough gems become better looking, finished products.

A potential phrase is, "Our service satisfies customers." This phrase might not be a home run, but it shows how our homework can easily produce a workable phrase. We started with the words "service" and "customer satisfaction," and we arrive at the above phrase without much effort. Part of this phrase's strength is the way it implies competitive services might not satisfy their customers.

Then, as you go over your customer interviews, you find out what makes them satisfied. It is the way your service ended the continually bad experience they had with your low-cost competitors. One customer told you, "The customer satisfaction your service provides costs a little more, but I believe I'm worth it."

Now with this you have the makings of a powerful phrase that you can place into various parts of your presentation. It can sound like this:

> We are not the least expensive service out there, nor will we ever be. If we went down that road we'd lose every customer we have. And here is why. I surveyed our customers to find out why they do business with us, and the consistent theme was they got tired of the bad service they were receiving. One customer put it like this: *Customer satisfaction costs a little more, and I'm worth it.* We slightly changed her words and made it our company's slogan: *Customer satisfaction costs a little more, and you're worth it.*

Repetition

As you keep using this message in different places within your presentation, stressing different points, it grows in emotional power.

Sales messages will never have the emotional power of Dr. Martin Luther King's great "I Have a Dream" speech. Somehow selling products just doesn't measure up to delivering civil rights to an oppressed minority. But his speech does illustrate many of the points I am trying to make.

He had a key phrase: *I have a dream*. His phrase is simple and short and expresses the powerful emotion of hope. Then, as he repeats it throughout his speech, it grows in emotional power. Here is a sampling of Dr. King's speech:

> I have a dream that one day this nation will rise up and live out the true meaning of its creed: "We hold these truths to be self-evident: that all men are created equal."
>
> I have a dream that one day on the red hills of Georgia the sons of former slaves and the sons of former slave owners will be able to sit down together at the table of brotherhood.
>
> I have a dream that one day even the state of Mississippi, a state sweltering with the heat of injustice, sweltering with the

heat of oppression, will be transformed into an oasis of freedom and justice.

I have a dream that my four little children will one day live in a nation where they will not be judged by the color of their skin but by the content of their character.

I have a dream today.

The phrases "content of their character" and "table of brotherhood," and even the borrowed sentence from the Declaration of Independence, support and augment his single, unifying phrase. Obviously, a sales message will need to be toned down considerably, but the phrases need to be targeted to the audience's heart in the same way Dr. King's were.

For example, phrases you use to support your unifying phrase can be borrowed. The phrase, "time is money," is a truism and it could be used as follows:

There is a saying, "time is money," and when you have to wait for the poor service others may have provided you in the past, the productivity losses mount. Customer dis-service is what I call bad customer service, and it takes a toll. But there is a better way, and it is called customer satisfaction. It costs a little more, and you're worth it.

As you repeat your phrase in different ways you emphasize different things. In the first example it was the way you removed customer discomfort caused by bad service. In this second example it emphasizes how bad service is ultimately expensive. But in every instance you are pounding home the message: we cost just a little more, not a lot more, and don't you think you're worth all the good things this small investment brings you?

Message Templates

Sometimes the phrase is the result of intoning three words that will resonate with the customer: "Simple, Reliable, Critical." In this example, the two sought after characteristics are followed by a word that emphasizes the absolute necessity of possessing them.

Other phrases that may resonate with customers are: "Designed for ____, by ____." In this template you simply fill in the blank with the decision maker's job description, "Designed for lawyers, by lawyers," or "Designed for doctors, by doctors." In other words, this product is just what you want, because the ones who designed it live in your world.

Conclusion

If words have emotional power, and they do, and emotions cause the buying decision, then shouldn't we spend a little time refining the words we use until we develop powerful stories and phrases? Use the presidential candidates as your guide. They have to sell a nation, which is no small task. They cause votes, in part, by using emotional phrases that define their campaign, and that are repeated throughout their campaigning in many different ways.

The great thing about stories and phrases is this: They don't have to be the products of your sales territory. If another territory produces a great story or phrase, then use it. After all, it is based on the same product.

Now it is time to go over some presentation techniques that will help make the words you use even more powerful.

9: Presentation Power

Developing a Script

Most salespeople speak off the top of their head. They don't want to appear scripted. Every presentation is their star turn at their own personal improv. They live for these moments on the stage.

That's selling, right? No. Selling is the art of causing a buying decision. So, if you are interested in closing sales, then I highly recommend scripting what you say so you don't appear like you are talking off the top of your head.

Let's compare the two approaches. Many of the benefits/solutions of your product offering can be complex. This complexity might cause an unscripted presenter to use 500 words to explain a solution. This is because we are not naturally succinct. Our sales pitch resembles a bag of dog food; much of it is filler.

The other approach involves writing a script for each presentation slide, or each demonstrated solution. This script initially comes off the top of our head. It is, therefore, likely to be wordy and lacking in punch. But after it is edited many times this 500-word mini-presentation is whittled down to 250 words. Powerful phrases are inserted, and the language is simple, easy to follow and tight.

Imagine multiplying the wordiness of Mr. Improv by thirty or more slides and compare it to the scripted approach that builds into its script repetition with variation, themes based on their emotional concerns, stories, phrases and so on. Which approach seems more powerful?

In the case of improvising, we have a tremendous amount of energy being released in an explosion. The energy moves outward in every direction, diffuse and unfocused. But when we script a presentation, this same amount of energy is focused like a laser beam at a specific target: generating emotions that close the sale.

I Don't Want to Look Like I Am Scripted

If there is an objection to this approach it is usually stated like this: "I will not appear natural; I will appear scripted."

My experience belies this objection. During our sales-training classes every instructor would be anonymously graded by the students on the content they delivered, and on their performance as a presenter. Even though every slide of my presentations was thoroughly scripted, I never once received the critique: "Tom appears too scripted." Instead, I was typically the highest rated instructor in class after class.

The students did not know my presentations were scripted, because I did not tell them, and here are the words of one student regarding the way my presentation style appeared: "Volcano under the ice flow. More energy than anyone I know under an amazingly calm exterior."

I believe this observation reflects what happens when a salesperson creates a powerful, well-edited message and knows it thoroughly. You are completely calm and collected on the outside yet the words you are speaking are bursting with energy. This is because all of the flabbiness of extemporaneous speech is gone. Your words are now muscular and compelling.

Concentrated Speech

What gives poetry its power? Part of the answer is the way it is so concentrated. In ten words, using the simplest language imaginable,

Shakespeare depicts the unforgettable moment of a man contemplating suicide:

> To be, or not to be—that is the question....[15]

Concentrated speech is powerful and it is difficult to speak in a concentrated fashion unless it is scripted. We will have fewer objections to this practice as we get a better sense of the impact of words. We need to think of them as having mass. When we multiply them unnecessarily they begin to weigh on the customer's mind. They become burdensome and tiresome. Therefore, it is important to keep our words to a minimum. Or, in the words of Strunk and White's *The Elements of Style*:

> A sentence should contain no unnecessary words, a paragraph no unnecessary sentences, for the same reason that a drawing should have no unnecessary lines and a machine no unnecessary parts. This requires not that the writer make all his sentences short, or that he avoid all detail and treat his subjects only in outline, but that every word tell.[16]

The words of Ecclesiastes were true then and are true today: "The more the words, the less the meaning, and how does that profit anyone?"[17]

Once we've scripted our presentation we need to rehearse this script to the point of memorizing it. Why? Because if we labor to remove unnecessary words, and develop a clean, simple sales message, then the last thing we want to do is throw this valuable message away and talk off the top of our head. And as we shall see, this extensive rehearsing will provide other benefits.

Prepare Their Minds, Provide Your Solution

If you are thirsty, then how satisfying is a glass of water on a scale of one to ten? It depends on how thirsty you are. If you were running

---

[15] William Shakespeare, *Hamlet,* Act III, Scene i, l. 56.
[16] Strunk & White, p. 23.
[17] Ecc 6:11, *The NIV Study Bible*, Kenneth Barker, Gen. Ed. (Grand Rapids: Zondervan Bible Publishers, 1985), p. 997.

in the 2007 Chicago Marathon, when some of the stations ran out of water, then I'm guessing that the marathoner who arrived at that empty station would have rated water as an "eleven" on the thirst-satisfaction scale that ranged from one to ten.

Stimulate thirst and one's appreciation of water increases. In sales this phenomenon translates into the following practice: Remind the customer of their painful experience before you present your solution, and you will increase the sales-impact of your solution

For example, let's suppose a customer experienced the following: A security alarm was loudly sounding every time a door was opened or closed during normal working hours. A day of this would have been unpleasant, but this problem continued intermittently for weeks. You bring back the memory of this nightmare just before you present your solution:

> When I surveyed your staff, I found the loud, balky system you are replacing caused a high level of frustration. Some said this problem contributed to a higher level of turnover. In other words, that loud, blaring noise was making your workplace unworkable for some. The good news is this will soon become a distant memory. Our system is the most reliable system on the market. For example, XYZ Inc. has had our system for four years and has yet to have one down day, or even call us for service.

Would it be powerful to mention how our installed product has yet to have one down day for four years and leave it at that? Of course, but it is emotionally more powerful to bring their maddening frustrations to the forefront of their minds, and then offer them the hope represented by your product. If I want a person to crave water, I give them salty snacks; I increase their thirst. If I want a customer to crave my solution, I remind them of the pain and suffering their problem caused them, or is causing them.

Constructing the Presentation

If you've ever had the opportunity to listen to a young preacher preach his first sermon, then you have probably seen the following. He makes about ten points instead of three, and he takes an hour to say what should have taken thirty minutes. Can a congregation possibly remember ten points? And can a diffuse presentation hold the audience's attention for that long?

When designing a solution for your decision makers, salespeople should be guided by this principle: *Ten to twenty points, made quickly, have no impact. They overwhelm the mind with details.* Therefore, pick out the few essential elements that the customer is looking for and lovingly linger over these points, embellish them with stories, testimonials, and the like.

Repetition with slight variations makes a message memorable. Advertising uses this approach because their mission is to sell products, and that won't happen if the listening audience forgets what their ads are saying.

Presentation Style: What Attention Span Problem?

There are many estimates of how long our attention can be held. Most of them are short—ten minutes or less—and I question them. It seems to me the attention-span problem is related to how interesting the information is, and how it is delivered. For example, when I look at a football fan the only thing that interrupts their laser-locked gaze is the overriding need to use the restroom. Outside of that, their intense stare is unwavering and they can later recall, in detail, the good and bad plays, and many of the plays in between.

What about the person who has a favorite TV program? When it comes on do they miss a lot of the program because they can't keep their minds from wandering? Or what about a great movie? Does it hold your attention for two hours? Yes, and you can discuss what it was about afterwards.

Now what do these scenarios have in common? Two things: Enjoyable content and an audio-visual medium featuring changes in scene, movement, color, sound, imagery and the like. Therefore, if you want to hold a customer's attention during your presentation, make it TV- or movie-like, and create interesting content.

The audio-visual element of television and movies is one of the reasons why I like PowerPoint. In a PowerPoint presentation I can embed videos, images, graphs, offer authoritative and footnoted citations, charts along with animation, and sound. Its TV-like quality helps me hold my customer's attention longer and I strive to make it as TV-like as possible.

When PowerPoint is abused the audience is subjected to a hail of bullet points that kills customer interest, and the fortunate drift into a narcoleptic coma to catch up on lost sleep. Bullet points are text-driven, and too many words can snow the most attentive minds. This is also known as: death by PowerPoint.

Comparing TV-Like to TV-Unlike

When I arrived at Small Midwestern I immediately noticed how my Region Managers were making presentations with lots of black and white slides crammed to the gills with text. The substance of their presentations was not the main problem, the style was.

One of my more influential Region Managers was having a hospital group visit our corporate office and I arranged the following presentation schedule. I would start our meeting with a thirty-minute presentation and he would have the remainder of the time.

When I gave my presentation with color, graphs, footnoted citations to clinical papers, animated sequences, and the like, the audience was enrapt. I then handed it over to my Region Manager. After ten minutes, while he was still talking, people began to stand up and leave to go to the restroom. The contrast between the two presentations was stark, and it was about to get even starker.

After he finished, and the presentation was over, a decision influencer came to me and asked for a copy of my presentation. I asked him why he wanted it. He said, "You've made my case for getting this system. You've got citations and illustrations that I can use to help sell this system internally." Wow! The presentation not only sold him, it co-opted him as a new salesperson for our company.

They did not ask for a copy of my Region Manager's presentation, and he, without being asked, radically overhauled his presentation's style.

Go over your current presentation and ask *is it more image-driven or text-driven*? If it is text-driven, then you need to start editing text out and adding visual illustrations in. One of the reasons why presentations have so much text is because it helps the presenter remember what to say. The following step takes away the need for this crutch.

Dancing Through the Minefield

When you are presenting, and are constantly being interrupted by a competitor's friend who is in the audience, how do you stay on task? How do you immediately get back into the flow of your presentation without missing a beat?

The Olympics offers us the answer. How can a figure skater fall during one of their high-degree-of-difficulty jumps and immediately get back into the flow of his or her program?

When you practice a skating routine hundreds of times your mind and muscles develop a memory for the moves, the music, one's location on the ice, and so on. The skater's ability to spring to their feet and continue as if their performance never experienced an interruption comes from hours of rehearsing.

Why does the U.S. Army spend millions of dollars on practicing war games? Because during the chaos of war a soldier will perform as he has trained. Bullets may be flying and bombs exploding, but the constant rehearsing generates a trained response that overcomes the disorientation caused by the battlefield.

I've given hundreds of sales presentations and I cannot remember one that was not rehearsed beforehand. If it was dramatically different from previous presentations, then I might rehearse it five to ten times. I did not need to rehearse this much to be good. But extensive rehearsing was required to master my material thoroughly. Now if a partisan sniped at me, their interruptions would not throw me off course.

Rehearsing also gave me a confidence that could be heard in the tone of my voice. When I spoke I wanted the customer to believe they were hearing the voice of an unassailable authority. This alone prevented most hecklers from speaking more than once.

Finally, my stories were told without a lot of unnecessary verbiage. My script was virtually memorized and the message was taut, muscular and flab-free. Also, my slides became less and less text dependent and more image-driven. I no longer needed the bullet-pointed sentences to remind me what I needed to say. If you do not rehearse extensively, then give it a try. For in a stressful and chaotic environment, salespeople will perform as they have trained.

Team Selling

He had just finished giving his third presentation to the same customer-group. He then looked up at me and said, "I'm all talked out. Do you have anything you want to say?"

"No," I said, because in more ways than one he had said all there was to say. The customer had probably stopped listening about fifteen minutes into his final presentation and my words would have only brought more pain to their longsuffering ears. Such is the fate of the Lone Ranger who tries to sell on his own.

Compare that to the person who used team selling. There were three presentations, and he never gave one of them by himself. During site visits he made sure I came along to help handle the customer group. He arranged for the company's engineers to be on a conference call with his customer's engineers. During the manufacturing visits he involved the CEO of the company and other officers.

When it was over, and the customer decided for our system, guess who got the credit for the sale? He did. Guess who got the commission? He did, and it was a big commission.

So why are salespeople so reluctant to bring in additional resources to help close big deals? Some don't trust others. Others don't want to share the limelight or the glory. But here is the funny thing about our team-selling sales star. To this day he is the only one who gets credit for closing this sale, and that is how it should be.

Team selling is becoming a necessity. Already many salespeople go on calls where the questions are so technical that an engineer, or even an engineering group from the home office, needs to be available to answer them. It is a skill worth mastering.

Final Presentation Tips

Always conduct a rehearsal before the presentation. You do not want to be prolix, pleonastic or periphrastic...that is, you don't want to be as pompous or wordy as this sentence is. But you do want to deliver differentiation messages in a calm, dispassionate voice. Rehearsing will make this possible even in hostile selling environments.

Finally, before you arrive, practice smiling and projecting an image of confidence and warmth. Your confidence will inspire trust and your warmth will make you appear accessible, and not aloof and remote.

A salesperson's work is not finished by the presentation. There is still much to be done, as we will discover in the section entitled: *Finishing Touches*.

Part Three:

Finishing Touches

10: The Mindset Of a Champion

If you've ever struggled to achieve something difficult then you know the battle is won within. You have to believe you can do it, or you won't attempt it. You have to want it badly and refuse to settle for anything less, or you will quit. You have to be willing to make sacrifices to achieve your goal, or you will fail to elevate your performance level to the degree necessary. Belief, desire and willingness do not come from the objective; they come from within where the battle for mastery is won.

We've discussed developing mindsets for our customers, because they influence their decisions and actions. Mindsets have the same affect on us; therefore, if a mindset can cause us to think or act in a certain way, and some of these thoughts and actions are associated with failure, then shouldn't we make it a priority to change our mindsets into ones associated with success?

The mindset of a champion is not about maintaining a positive mental attitude, or self-belief, or visualizing success. It is about understanding how we are wired, and developing mindsets that counter our unhealthy tendencies.

A champion's mindset refuses to accept what is easy and natural, because more often than not, the path of least resistance is mediocrity's highway. Therefore, the champion finds herself adopting attitudes that are the exact opposite of what is commonly held. Among the attitudes she rejects are those most have about constant, rapid, unsettling change.

Constant Change Is Disorienting

We live in a world of *Future Shock* according to the famous futurist, Alvin Toffler, who wrote a book with that title. Future Shock is a world where there are so many changes occurring so quickly that the mind is overwhelmed.

I have one response to the overwhelmed: Future Shock is for wimps. Yes, change is occurring more and more rapidly. You cannot change this fact. You, therefore, have a choice: embrace change or be steamrolled by it.

Change is occurring much faster these days and technology is a driver of it. We've gone from faxes and pagers, to cell phones and email, to tweeting, texting, smart phones, iPads and social networking in a very short period.

Do we really think this sort of rapid change will slow down? Every indication suggests the pace of change will continue to accelerate, and with these tectonic shifts in technology comes an ever-changing customer. Unless we are constantly changing, our customers will leave us behind.

The Fast-Changing Sales Environment

When I arrived at Small Midwestern the decision maker for our product was the Facilities Engineer. He had also been the decision maker for more than thirty years. But nurses were coming to the fore and asserting their power. After they became the decision-making force, many salespeople were still selling in a way that appealed primarily to Facilities Engineers.

Who could blame them? A habit reinforced by thirty years of activity is not easy to break, but it had to be broken and it was. This change in decision makers required us to change everything about our presentation.

Then, about four-to-five years later, the decision became more IT-influenced. This resulted in another radical change in how we sold our product. Now IT is, in many cases, the decision maker. For thirty years the decision maker was the same, and then it changed three times in ten years. With every change an enormous amount of work was required to adapt to the new situation.

This effort that change requires is one of the reasons why we resist changing and remain creatures of habit. We love our routines. It is a trait shared by virtually everyone. It is the easy path. That is why the salesperson who loves change has a decided advantage. Her competitors may not be willing to invest the effort until failure forces their hand. Meanwhile, while they delayed changing, the champion has changed many times and is, once again, a step ahead of her competitors.

Sometimes it is difficult to change your sales approach. You've done it ten times before, but now you've run out of ideas. If that is the case, then bring in outside help to create a new message. But whatever you do, do not tell the same old story, or sing the same old song, because your competitors will find ways to neutralize the power of your message, and force you to change your tune.

Also, if a salesforce tells the same message for too long, they get bored with it, and their boredom shows in presentations devoid of enthusiasm. When selling becomes a chore for us, imagine what a chore it becomes for our customers.

Embrace Change

To embrace change we need to redefine it. Instead of thinking, "How can I change?" think, "How can I improve?" Continuous improvement requires constant modification or change.

Once the attitude is changed, then the desired behaviors are more likely to follow. Review your presentation every quarter and ask questions like: "How can I make it more emotionally powerful? What are the weakest parts of the presentation that I need to strengthen? Has the competition repositioned themselves in a way that makes my presentation weaker and, if so, how do I change my presentation to overcome this?"

Your goal needs to be to improve how you sell each quarter, if not each week. The change can be great or small, but some change needs to be introduced, or else you will grow comfortable in your rut and will soon become a standing target instead of a moving one.

Change is the enemy of complacency and the status quo. It is the enemy of mindsets, the mental guardian of the status quo. Think about it: What does a mindset do? It keeps us thinking in the same way. New inputs are assimilated to fit the existing image. Mindsets resist change. They can blind us to what is really happening in the world.

This is what makes embracing change an important characteristic of a champion, because we cannot escape mindsets. They form whether we want them to or not. But a champion who embraces change can govern, to a degree, that which will otherwise govern her. Rather than be subject to the mindset's tendency to continue seeing things in the same way, a champion will constantly look for ways she can change her viewpoint, understanding and practices for the better.

However, the world of sales is mostly behavioral, and when we sell we cannot see our behaviors. What is obvious to outside observers is not so obvious to us. Since we cannot see what needs improving, a champion embraces another strange attitude: constructive criticism is good, and I seek it.

Seek Constructive Criticism

The best golfers in the world turn to coaches to work on the mechanics of their swing. No one forces them to go to a coach to receive a critique; they seek it out because they want to improve. Like professional golfers, we need to become seekers of coaching, because it accelerates our improvement.

I did my best to impart a love of criticism during our sales training program. The students would have to make a sales presentation on the first day of training based on a scenario they were sent in advance. Their performance was then videotaped and subjected to an extensive critiquing process that went like this:

After their presentation, they would get the opportunity to critique themselves. First, they were to tell us what they liked about their presentation. Then they could tell us what they thought they needed to improve. Whatever they pointed out in the critique was now off the table for discussion, because they obviously knew they needed to perform better in this area.

Next, their peers would critique them. Again, this session began with telling the salesperson what they were doing well. Also, the students needed to be accurate in their criticism because they would have their turn in a few minutes. Harsh, pointed criticism almost never occurred. Virtually all were respectful and were motivated by a strong desire to help their peer.

A Region Manager, or two, would first praise and then critique the student, and then I would praise and critique them to cover anything that might have been missed.

This critiquing process extended to the other trainers and me. Everyday, after every training session, we would be anonymously critiqued by the class. They even got to critique the critiques we gave them. Each instructor and each module would receive a numerical score and comments. These scores and comments were then summarized and published company wide.

On the final day of the class the students gave a second presentation. It received the same critiquing as the first day's presentation, and it was videotaped. The level of improvement these videotapes chronicled was amazing, and that was the primary point of the videotaping. It demonstrated how dramatically someone's sales performance could improve over a short period of time when their focus was on behaviors that cause a buying decision. It also revealed how criticism is the path of accelerated growth and improvement. It is not to be feared, but embraced.

Grunt Work Does Not Exist

Not all sales tasks are created equal. The presentation is, for most salespeople, the narcotic that keeps them hooked on selling. They get to play before an audience and find out just how much their performance was appreciated.

That's great. I would never diminish that fun and exciting part of the job. But if a salesperson fails to perform the less-glorious tasks, like prospecting, because they view it as grunt work, then an attitude adjustment is in order. There is no such thing as grunt work in sales. There is work that causes sales success, and work that doesn't. The successful salesperson focuses on what causes sales success, and disregards what doesn't. [Note: this does not mean salespeople disregard administrative requirements like call reports, etc.]

We cannot let our attitudes defeat us. Incorrect attitudes toward work are the enemy within that can beat us more easily than any competitor. And if I disdain doing what causes sales to close, then my attitude toward these tasks needs to change.

One of the ways to change an attitude about something is to understand it better. Simplify what you are looking at, and it becomes easier to see it and judge its value. Prospecting is simply this: a practice conferring some of the greatest sales advantages there are.

These new mindsets that embrace change, criticism and "grunt" work will help us in sales and in life. And when we combine them with a philosophy of simplicity we will have a winning combination, for it is through the mental discipline of simplifying problems that the keys to many mazes can be found.

To Simplify Is to Understand

To simplify is to understand. We cannot get our arms around needless complexity. We chase down its rabbit trails and it leads us back to where we started. There is only one way of defeating complexity and that is to ignore its thousands of questions and answers, its million half-truths, and reduce it to its essence. When the complex is distilled to its simplest terms it becomes definable, understandable, and a treasure house of revelation.

We underestimate the value of simplicity. However, when confronted by complex issues, problems, opportunities—call them

The Mindset of a Champion

what you will—simplifying matters should be our first and most pressing concern. The following example shows how powerful simplifying a complex issue can be.

President Ronald Reagan faced one of the most complex problems any president has ever faced: The Cold War struggle with the Soviet Union. The Soviet Union, as Russia was then called, was active in countries throughout the world, supporting some regimes and undermining others. They oppressed a host of satellite nations, had a massive army and a nuclear arsenal. Their spies penetrated the deepest levels of our intelligence agencies. It is difficult to imagine a more complex challenge. The key to successfully meeting this challenge was to distill it to its simplest form.

The following story is from Richard Allen, who served under Mr. Reagan as the Director of the National Security Agency:

> In January 1977, I visited Ronald Reagan in Los Angeles. During our four-hour conversation, he said many memorable things, but none more significant than this. "My idea of American policy toward the Soviet Union is simple, and some would say simplistic," he said. "It is this: We win and they lose. What do you think of that?" One had never heard such words from the lips of a major political figure; until then we had thought only in terms of *managing* the relationship with the Soviet Union.
>
> Reagan went right to the heart of the matter. Utilizing American values, strength, and creativity, he believed we could outdistance the Soviets and cause them to withdraw from the Cold War or perhaps even to collapse.[18]

In retrospect, his simplification of the problem may seem unremarkable, but for the time it was a quantum leap in our understanding of how to fight the Cold War. By distilling this complex problem down to its essential element—in war, you win or

---

[18] Richard Allan, *The Man Who Won the Cold War* (Hoover Digest, 2000, No. 1, The Fall of Communism). The on-line link to this article is: http://www.hoover.org/publications/hoover-digest/article/7398

lose—he was able to transform the way the U.S. participated in the Cold War, and this led to our winning it.

No matter what your profession, no matter what your role, your performance will benefit greatly from a mindset that holds simplicity to be a top priority. By simplifying a task to its central, defining points you uncover the one or two areas that deserve all of your attention. The following will show how simplifying things led to our sales success at Small Midwestern, and the creation of this book.

Simplify Your Business

When I arrived at Small Midwestern I wanted to know the answer to one question, "What are the most important causes of sales growth?" Ultimately I narrowed my focus to two things:

1. Coverage: The number of salespeople working in large markets, and the number of hours a distributor sales force dedicated to our product.

2. Competence: The selling skills of our distributor salespeople.

Where our distributors were too thin in their representation we struggled, and many of the largest markets suffered from this. Where our distributor salespeople were excellent we did well, and several were remarkably talented. But where they were woeful no amount of corporate assistance in the field could help. This is because we were competing against the polished salespeople from Fortune 500 companies. The customer looked at the Fortune 500 sales professional and felt comfortable, and then looked at one of the weak distributor salespeople and feared being associated with us in any way. This led to the development of our sales training course.

As I worked on developing the modules for this course, I again tried to boil sales down to its simplest principles. When I finally realized how the sale was caused by emotions, it led me to analyze every aspect of our sales process to see if it reflected this understanding. By reducing sales to its simplest component—the causes of the buying-decision-effect—I was able to understand better how this complex sales process works.

This simplifying thought-process needs to be adopted by salespeople as well. Before rushing to employ these ideas, or any others, a salesperson should think, "What is the most important thing I need to be doing to grow my sales?" Her concern should not be about what is important for tomorrow, or this quarter, but for her career. There may be ten things begging for attention, but do not cast them a glance; focus, instead, on the most important thing.

Don't rush to a conclusion. Test whatever you come up with. Think about it. Weigh it. Then do it.

Occam's Razor and Thoreau

During the Middle Ages there was a philosopher, William of Occam, who is credited with the insight known as Occam's Razor, or the Law of Parsimony. It states that when you have competing explanations, the one with the fewest assumptions, the simplest one, should be chosen.

We would be wise to apply this simplifying approach to our speech (fewer words), our presentations (fewer themes), our products (less complexity), and our life. As Henry David Thoreau once wrote in *Walden*:

> Our life is frittered away by detail. ... Simplicity, simplicity, simplicity! I say, let your affairs be as two or three, and not a hundred or a thousand; instead of a million count half a dozen, and keep your accounts on your thumb-nail.[19]

The successful salesperson focuses on that which causes success and, by eliminating the extraneous interests competing for her time, her success becomes much more likely. One area of focus is on her relationships with key customers, for without them, she goes nowhere.

---

[19] Henry D. Thoreau, *The Annotated Walden,* ed. Philip Van Doren Stern (New York: Clarkson N. Potter, Inc. 1970), p. 222.

11. Relationships

The Market We Never Cracked

There was one small part of the country where we never seemed to get any business. A salesperson who had faithfully serviced his customers for over twenty years had a virtually impenetrable territory. He wasn't much to look at, but his customers seemed to put little stock in matinee-idol looks. However, he did bring value to the equation. When his customers got in a jam, he was on the problem and tended to produce immediate results.

He developed a bond of trust that was, to his customers, more important than what his product was or did. If his product could do the job reasonably well, then they wanted it from him, because he came with the product.

What was the cause of his sales success? He was. His product was one of the worst in the market. Its market share was negligible, except in his market. There was no logical reason for customers to keep buying it. It was essentially throwing money away for the privilege of owning outmoded technology. But they stayed faithful to their salesperson because he had become a valued member of their team. He was family. His entire career was a confirmation of the way emotions cause sales decisions.

I never had the chance to sell against him. Had I sold against him I am confident of the outcome: I would have lost. The reason why is because the customer was not in the market for a product, and all I was selling was a product. They were in the market to preserve a business relationship, and this shows how relationships can become the deciding factor in a selling situation. His relationships were giving him an unassailable competitive advantage.

Relationships and Their Downside

How a customer feels about their salesperson is one of the more powerful determinants of sales success. If they love, respect and trust you, then they want to give you their business and will even protect it from competitors. When a competitor comes prowling around the customer will not only inform their salesperson, they will also steer the competitor away from the account.

However, there is a problem with developing and maintaining strong relationships: They take time. What if you have 100 accounts, and each account has three important department heads who make decisions about your products? How will you be able to develop 300 strong relationships?

It's virtually impossible, particularly when you factor in the turnover that will occur. As soon as you develop 150 relationships over a period of years you may discover that 50 of them are now gone through turnover. This points to the need for a plan that conserves the precious resource of a salesperson's time, and makes strong relationships at key accounts.

Step One: Apply the 80-20 Rule

Have you ever noticed how weird the 80-20 rule is? It applies to a wide variety of tasks that are completely unrelated. The man who developed this rule, the Italian economist, Vilfredo Pareto, based it on the following discoveries: 20% of the pea pods in his garden contained 80% of the peas. He then observed how 80% of the land in Italy was owned by 20% of the population. When he surveyed other countries he found a similar percentage applied. Like I said, weird.

In sales, this percentage often turns up as follows: 20% of your accounts will contribute 80% of your business. Don't ask me why it works, it just does. If it works for pea pods and land ownership, then surely it can work for sales. Sales managers have long applied this rule in managing salespeople.

The Pareto Principle, or the 80-20 rule, focuses the salesperson on developing relationships at his top accounts. If he has a territory of 100 accounts, then he focuses on those 20 accounts that are the largest potential producers of business in his market. If there are approximately three decision makers at each account, this reduces the number of relationships he has to develop to a manageable 60 instead of an unmanageable 300.

This does not mean he will treat the other customers with less courtesy, or will fail to take care of their problems and concerns as they arise. It does mean he will not be spending as much time at his smaller accounts developing relationships.

Step Two: Get to Know Them

Communication Preferences

Get to know your customer. This step is not as obvious as it appears. It goes beyond knowing their birthdays, their kid's birthdays, and the personal details that give dimension to a relationship. It goes much deeper.

Everyone prefers a communication style, and we are most comfortable with communication styles that are similar to our own. For example, two quiet people could happily speak to each other for hours, but a loud and boisterous person would likely set a quiet person's teeth on edge. By recognizing our customer's communication style preference, and modifying ours to mesh better with theirs, we can increase a customer's comfort level and speed up the relationship-building process.[20]

So how do we discover the communication preferences of others, or our own for that matter? The Myers-Briggs Type Indicator® (MBTI®) is a tool providing these insights. We will first look briefly

---

[20] This material on MBTI® is taken from the chapter on Emotional Intelligence in my book entitled, *No Medal for Second Place: How to Finish First in Job Interviews*. To preview this book go to www.nomedalforsecondplace.com.

at the history and the theory, and then examine the behaviors associated with different types.

History

The starting point for this theory was the work of Carl Jung, a Swiss psychiatrist who studied under Sigmund Freud. He split with Freud and developed a different theory of personality based on types. Introverts and extraverts are two well-known types that his theory introduced to the world's vocabulary. They form a dichotomy, or a contrast of opposites, one of three he developed to explain the personality.

The mother-daughter team of Katherine Cook Briggs and Isabel Briggs Myers added a fourth dichotomy; they also developed a self-reporting tool to help people discover their psychological type.

The Four Dichotomies

According to this theory, there are four dichotomies and our preference for one category over another produces our four-letter type. These categories, and the associated letters, are:

1. Extraversion-Introversion, or E-I
2. Sensing-Intuition, or S-N (Intuition is represented by the letter "N," because the letter "I" was already taken by Introversion)
3. Thinking-Feeling, T-F
4. Judging-Perceiving, J-P (added by Myers-Briggs)

The following is an oversimplification of how our preferences produce a four-letter type: An extravert (E), who gathers information through the senses (S), makes decisions logically (T), and prefers delaying the completion of tasks to the last minute (P), is an ESTP.

Throughout our lives we operate in all eight of the above categories, but we prefer to operate in one dichotomy-category over another. An extravert, for example, is capable of introverted activity, and engages in it throughout his life, but it is not his preferred mode of operation.

The Causes of Sales Success

This may seem complicated—and it can be—until we reduce this theory to some of its behavioral elements. Once we do this, we will find ourselves examining just two sets of behavioral preferences. The first set is the preference for judging or perceiving.

(A brief aside: Some of the names for these dichotomies can be confusing. For example, if your preferred way of dealing with the outer world is through judging this doesn't mean you are judgmental. And if your preference is perceiving, then this doesn't mean you are more perceptive.)

Judging and Perceiving

The judging type deals with the world by imposing order on it. He is more scheduled, methodical and organized than the perceiving type, and prefers to drive things to closure rather than leave tasks undecided and open-ended. Finishing tasks energizes the judging type. He is almost never late for an appointment and is often early.

In the world of communication style, a judger can grow impatient with people who take too long to get to the point. If you ramble on about the sports, weather, your dog or cat, you will drive up his discomfort level and delay, or destroy, your attempt to build a strong relationship.

The perceiving type approaches the world in the opposite fashion. He is less structured, more spontaneous, adaptable, open-ended, and not concerned with rushing things to their desired end. He can be late for appointments and never be bothered by it, something unfathomable to many judging types.

But do not think perceivers are the ones who are always late and never finish a project on time. They can be every bit as effective at successfully finishing projects as the judging types, but they tend to do it at the last minute. Why? In part, because they want to gather as much new information as possible, since it may result in a better decision, but also because they are energized by the pressure of a deadline.

The judgers prefer people to get to the point. Their mindset is, "I asked you what time it was. I didn't ask you to build me a clock." They are typically more assertive than the perceiving type and will

Relationships

interrupt you to get to the point. We can recognize the judging type during a sales call by their business-like approach. Not much time will be wasted on chitchat. They may ask, "How was traffic?" And with that the pleasantries end and the business conversation begins. Finally, they tend to be more focused and intense in their appearance than most perceivers.

The perceiving types are more casual and relaxed in their appearance. They enjoy processing information. They will engage in chitchat and ask you about your recent vacation, something a judger is not likely to do until after a strong relationship has been built. With perceivers it is best to relax and go with the flow. To continually try to steer them back to your business objective, when they would rather explore a different topic, is to make them uncomfortable.

With this dichotomy we have a clear illustration of potential communication problems based on one's communication style.

Extraverts and Introverts

The extravert-introvert dichotomy is perhaps the most misunderstood. We tend to think of extraverts as the outgoing type who loves interacting with people while the introverts are shy, retiring wallflowers, but this view is inaccurate.

This dichotomy refers to the way these two types direct their energy and receive it. Extraverts direct their energy toward the external world of things and people. This means they have less energy available for the inner world of thought and contemplation. Introverts are the exact opposite. They direct their energy toward the inner world of thought and reflection and consequently have less energy for the outer world of people and things.

These types also *receive* energy from their external or internal orientations. An introvert can spend hours, or days, thinking about a problem that needs solving. They are energized by this activity, while an extravert would likely be drained by it.

Extraverts *tend* to be more expressive than introverts. They prefer interacting with others and the environment to being alone in the world of ideas and thoughts. They tend to speak faster and are more likely to interrupt. They are often more animated, action-oriented and sociable. They prefer to talk things out and this shows how even their thought process has an externalized, action-orientation.

These behaviors suggest the extraverted customer would not feel as comfortable with someone whose quieter behaviors suggested a low-energy level. Since people tend to judge others according to the gold standard of themselves, the extravert might find the quieter type uninteresting. After all, an introvert's special gifts are introverted, or hidden to the outside world. They are often underestimated because of this. Because we prefer a communication style similar to our own, it is wise to mirror, to a degree, the behavioral expression of the customer. But don't over do it or people will think you are a fake.

If you have an extremely expressive personality, then, when you are around an introverted customer, toning down its wattage is a good idea. I know some extraverts who are so intense and expressive that they are overwhelming to other extraverts; so imagine how uncomfortable extremely extraverted behaviors can make some introverted customers feel. Would you seek a relationship with someone who strums your nerves like a banjo string?

Objection

Some may feel this sort of behavior modification is verging on losing one's identity and becoming a fraud. I disagree. When a person is hard of hearing, I raise my voice so they can hear me. I modify my behavior to be heard. Is that fraud? I normally don't speak with a booming voice, but the situation required it, and the other person appreciated my accommodating his communication needs. I am doing the same thing with a customer when I, for example, intentionally get to the point much faster than normal. I am simply modifying my behavior to accommodate his communication needs.

Sensing and Intuition, Thinking and Feeling

The remaining four MBTI® categories are not as important when it comes to our communication style, because they are not as behavioral. In sales, our focus is behavior, because it generates perceptions and mindsets that generate emotions that cause closed sales. The last four type categories are not as behavioral because

Relationships

they are mental functions; they are primarily concerned with the internal world of gathering information (perception), and making decisions (judgment).[21]

Emotional Map

Perhaps the most important thing one can do in this relationship building phase is determine what moves the decision makers and influencers emotionally. If they currently use your product and love it, why is that? Also, what annoys them about other products and services? What are their hopes and fears? What is their boss tasking them to do for this year, and are these goals radically different from past years?

Determine who will be the likely decision makers for your product, or service, and the typical influencers. It can vary slightly from account to account so your guesses might be off, but you will still get a sense for where your customer is headed, what they are trying to achieve, and what they find threatening and bothersome.

Avocations

What do your customers love doing in their spare time? Golf, garden, cook, run, Pilates, read mysteries, travel, whatever it is, find out about it. Then, instead of sending them professional articles, send them recipes, articles on golf or running, scoops on hot new travel destinations, and the like. Your correspondence is welcomed, because these subjects appeal strongly to your customer.

As you develop your database you may find out there are peers who work in same industry, or profession, and share the same avocation. If so, then put the two in touch with each other:

> Hey Jim, do you know John Smith? No? Anyway, he has the same position as you at XYZ, Inc. and he is also passionate about golfing. Every vacation is a golfing vacation. You

---

[21] These four mental functions are, however, critical when it comes to teambuilding, leadership, managing conflict, and other important activities within an organization. I use the entire MBTI model in my management consulting. For more information go to www.essentialgrowthsolutions.com.

ought to look him up at the next [statewide professional meeting, industry event, etc.] and compare notes.

Then, when these two golfers meet, they will have something of great interest to talk about, and one of their topics will likely be how you are one of their favorite salespeople.

Step Three: Prove Yourself
Developing the Bond of Trust

What is the basis of a relationship? Trust. If someone does not trust you, then the foundation upon which a relationship is formed is missing. For the salesperson that is trying to establish strong, positive relationships, this trust-factor is enormously important.

Since our entire sales approach is behavior based, what behaviors can nurture the bond of trust? One simple behavior is returning calls immediately.

Think about it. Your customer is stressed, time-starved, burdened by a to-do list that only seems to grow and never shrink. If you are the one person who always gets back in touch with them in minutes instead of hours or days, then you become someone they can rely on. Reliability and trust are strongly linked: If I can't rely on you, then how can I trust you? If I trust you, then aren't I relying on you?

This simple behavior is not as easy to adopt as you might think. Over 100 things occur in a busy salesperson's day and stand in the way of this. The demands of travel, meetings, presentations, and so on, can delay a returned phone call. This means a salesperson must be disciplined and develop a new mindset about following up quickly with customers. Cultivate the belief that a call returned in minutes is as powerful a cause of sales success as is a good sales presentation.

Armed with this attitude your behaviors should change. During all-day meetings you will check for messages at each break, and any calls you've received will be returned immediately. Unless it's an emergency, you might not be able to satisfy their need, but that is not what is critical. The most important part of this exercise is simply to return the call as soon as possible, because it shows the customer just how much he or she matters to you. The unspoken message that the customer hears is, "When I call, my salesperson drops everything to see what I need."

In some respects this simple behavior resembles the courtship behaviors covered in Chapter Two. It shows the customer they are the center of your universe. And it will likely differentiate you from your competitors, because few others make the effort to do this. It is so much easier to wait until the end of the day and then return calls, or call back the next day; and this is what they are used to. Therefore, this behavior will likely separate you from your competitors. It also shows you are reliable, therefore, worthy of trust.

Job Security

We live in troubling economic times. Europe appears to be on the verge of collapsing beneath the weight of unsustainable public sector spending. The U.S., with its annual trillion $ deficits, seems to be writing a script for its own Greek tragedy. Joblessness is a global problem. Fear may be an irrational emotion, but during these times it seems like a reasonable response.

If you are in sales, take heart. The salesperson who is loved by his customers is the person who has one of the safest jobs in the world. Yes, it is true that companies sometimes terminate the employment of incredibly good salespeople, and make many other bad decisions as well. But even those excellent salespeople who are terminated are typically safe, because they possess what other companies will gladly hire them for: access to their relationships.

Job security in this time of economic uncertainty and high unemployment is something most people prize. One of the best ways to achieve it in sales is through developing strong relationships, because no thoughtful company would want to lose such a salesperson to the competition.

Final Notes

You need to plan outcomes, but you also need to enjoy what is unplanned. As you start this process of developing relationships you will meet people with whom you have little in common, some may be off-putting, but many others will become true friends. This is one of the most satisfying aspects of a sales career.

Yes, you are planning on developing relationships, but this does not mean that each and every one of them won't be authentic and meaningful. We should not view this relationship-building exercise as work, but as an investment in enjoyment. People are what make the sales career fulfilling, so move forward in that spirit and—with a nod to Dale Carnegie—you will win friends and influence people.

Now that you have dozens of customer-friends who have given you their business it is time to move on to new fields of conquest, right? Not exactly. There is still a lot of work to be done after the sale.

12: After the Sale

If you were told about the strongest possible cause of a buying decision, stronger than differentiation, would you utilize it? You would if you could, but not all salespeople can. That is because this technique requires an appreciative, very satisfied customer, and not every salesperson has one.

What makes a customer satisfied? What happens after the sale is one of the strongest determinants of customer satisfaction, and this area is typically neglected. This is because companies oftentimes have other departments looking after the delivery, installation, training of customers and servicing of products. But whether or not the salesperson is obligated to stay involved after the sale (perhaps for in-servicing customers), he still needs to make certain he takes an active role in the after-sale activities for several important reasons. One reason is to make sure none of his customers become dissatisfied.

Dissatisfied Customers

We were trying our best to close a deal with a new hospital. We were now the market-share leading company in our space, but the customer wanted state of the art from companies with name recognition. Our technology was proven but dated, and our name recognition was still negligible. When one of our large, well-known competitors came out with a new system, they immediately became the frontrunner.

The customer's mindset favored our competitor. What could we do? We had to change their mindset into one that favored us by convincing them that the decision they made was: Buy a system that works or buy one that doesn't. Our research told us that our competitor's beta site for their new product was buggier than a sewer in Calcutta. The hospital where the beta site was installed was threatening to yank it out. Obviously our competitor was not letting these facts stand in the way of telling the customer just how great their new system was.

What could we do? We spent the last fifteen minutes of our presentation pleading with the customer to visit the one place where this new system was installed. Unfortunately, this would require them to fly over 1,000 miles.

Now who would go to this trouble? A person that feared making a multi-million dollar mistake. As we told them, "If you have to pull out their system and install ours you will spend more than twice the amount that you should. And we would not go to the trouble of asking a potential customer to inconvenience themselves if we were not fairly certain that their current product is incapable of doing what they now claim it can."

They visited this hospital on a Friday. The following week we had a contract to install our system.

The power of a negative reference is considerable, and this provides us with another incentive to aim for only satisfied customers. However, the negative reference is tricky. If a competitor has a widespread reputation for excellence, then supplying a solitary, negative reference can make you look like a dishonest basher. Therefore, be judicious in the use of them. They can backfire on you if they do not reflect the overall picture.

Tactics Leading to a Strategic Goal

"What leads to customer satisfaction?" One powerful cause is the way your product delivers on its promise by solving the problems you claimed it would. If it fails to live up to its promise, then your customer may feel they were sold a bill of goods.

Behavior Change

What stands in the way of products and services delivering on their promises are typically not misrepresentations from dishonest salespeople, but the need for the customer to adopt new behaviors to use the product properly, which is never easy.

What drives behavior changes in organizations? Most organizations have workers, managers and upper management. For example, in the U.S. Army there are the privates who do the work, the sergeants who supervise it and make sure it gets done, and the officers who lead. Now of these three groups of people which one is best suited to drive behavior change? Ask any private and the answer is, "The sergeants drive behavior change." The same is true in the corporate setting. The first line supervisors, or managers, are the ones who are best suited to change the behavior of their team.

Therefore, all corporate training programs must develop and train *all* of these trainers. Absent their involvement, the necessary behavior change typically fails to take place throughout their organization, and the wonderful promises of your product remain unfulfilled.

Most corporations realize the need to train trainers, but they implement it in a piece-meal fashion. For example, they might train a few super-users, or a group of trainers, when their goal should be to train *all* first-level supervisors who will use their product. To the degree that a company is able, their product or service should be customized to fit the work habits of these supervisors—now it is their system—and after it is installed and goes live, it is important to work with them over the next few days to make sure the training sticks.

We tend to sell upper management, train the workers, and forget about the very people who are ideally suited to drive the behavior change every new system requires. When a system focuses on training all first-line supervisors the results can be amazing.[22]

---

[22] These ideas come largely from Kaye Verner who developed and implemented a nurse-training program that produced remarkable results.

Follow-Up

If a product or service requires training, the salesperson should be there for at least the first day, and longer if things don't go well. The customer needs to feel they have an advocate within the company who will speak up for them in the event of training miscues and difficulties. But let's assume all went well, is the salesperson's job finished?

Yes, for the moment, because you don't want to be a pest, and you do have other sales tasks to accomplish. But always remember that a salesperson can benefit from a satisfied customer more than anyone else. Therefore, the salesperson should care more about that customer's satisfaction than anyone else.

After the product is successfully implemented, the salesperson should secure an appointment to return about a week later to make sure the behavior change is taking hold. If it's not, then you need to see about arranging supplemental training at no additional charge. There will never be a better time to train the customer than in the days after the product is delivered. If the customer's behavior change is still evident after a week, then set an appointment to stop by a month later. While there, see if your product is generating any new success stories you can use in future presentations.

Let's say your product is so easy that it always gets installed without a hitch. Should you be there when it is delivered? Yes, because the purpose of this exercise is to show the decision maker that you truly care about their satisfaction. It matters to you. Nothing can convincingly demonstrate this as much as your investment of time.

The Satisfied Customer's Impact

Goal number one: turn your customers into salespeople who are happy to represent your product to potential customers.

When it comes to selling, the passionate testimony of satisfied customers is more powerful than anything. The reasons why are:

1. They are a trusted, unbiased source of information. They are not paid to represent this product.

2. The satisfied customer can authoritatively answer questions that quiet the prospect's fears: How long did it take your staff to get used to this product? Are you glad you bought it? They say their product can do this, does it? How well do they service your account?

3. A customer's testimony can establish the trustworthiness of a salesperson, his company and his product.

4. Salespeople don't live in the customer's world. No salesperson has a day-in, day-out, end-user experience of their product like a customer does.

I've been to territories where there was not one satisfied customer reference to give to an account that wanted at least three. Now if the competitor produced a list of three who were strong supporters and were local, and our team produced three references from out of state, then what will the customer conclude? Two things:

1. The product must be okay if it can produce satisfied customers in other markets.

2. This salesperson must provide such horrible service that he does not have even one satisfied customer.

The inability to produce a single, local reference is a red flag no salesperson should fly.

Leveraging Your Assets

How do we take advantage of this powerful asset?

First, don't wait to be asked for a reference. If a prospect-group—the decision maker and influencers—is considering your product, then offer to pick them up and take them to your reference account. Since you are in control of the process, advise the prospect, "They have 11 AM to 12 noon available on the following days. Which day works best?" After they pick the day you let them know that the lunch that follows is an important part of the process, because it allows you to discuss what was shown, answer questions and discuss next steps, if any.

The Causes of Sales Success

When you enter the site, a representative from your satisfied customer should be waiting in the lobby to guide the prospect-group to a meeting with their peers—if the CIO is the decision maker, then he meets with the CIO. The sales team stays behind in the lobby, because the power of this meeting comes from your prospect's unfettered access to someone who is in love with your product, your company and you.

The prospect-group gets to speak freely with the satisfied customers for around an hour, are shown the product in operation, are told what the customer was promised and what they received, how they've been treated on the back end, and so on. Then the prospect-group and sales team meets in the lobby around noon to go to lunch.

At lunch the salesperson asks: Are there any remaining concerns? Did you see how easy it was for the staff to use this product? Were you shown how the product was customized to fit their unique needs? The goal is to make sure the visit was a success that covered the bases. Yes, you will have coached your satisfied customer to make sure they mention a few important things, and to speak freely, but sometimes meetings don't happen exactly as we would like them too, and you need to make sure all of the important points were covered.

You then discuss what the next steps are over a nice meal while a positive emotional connection is being forged between you and your future customer.

The impact of these tours cannot be overestimated. Peer-to-peer selling is by far the most persuasive type of selling. However, since this requires your satisfied customer to take time out of their busy schedule it should only be used for the larger opportunities, and only a few times a year, otherwise you can burn out a reference account.

Such customers who go the extra mile for you deserve special treatment. It could be something as simple as catering a lunch with pizzas for their staff, but somehow—within the confines of their policies and in accord with their wishes—thanks need to be expressed.

Conclusion

If your customers are not satisfied, then your chances of success are weakened as a result. Their satisfaction needs to be a primary goal of the salesperson and the corporation, because no salesperson can, on their own, do everything needed to satisfy a customer. Too many departments are involved in their ultimate satisfaction: Shipping, installing, training, customer service, and so on. But here is what the salesperson can do. He can be his customer's advocate, and intervene on their behalf when things fall short.

The Next Chapter

What follows is a guideline on what sales performance coaching should look like, but often does not. If you are a salesperson, you should read this chapter. Then, if you can see the potential benefits of this system, you might want to loan your book to your boss.

13. Sales Performance Coaching

Typical, Ineffective Coaching

I was traveling with my sales manager and one of his salespeople. I told my sales manager what the purpose of my visit was. I wanted to see his salesperson in a sales situation, and then observe his—my sales manager's—sales performance coaching at the end of the call.

The salesperson met with the customer and made nice for five or ten minutes and then left. The sales performance coach then launched into his typical spiel: "Great call! Great call!!! I really liked the way you established an immediate rapport with the customer and asked him to make sure to keep you in mind when it comes time for him to order. Now he knows what we're all about as a company. We stand ready to serve. Great call!"

Good grief.

Sales performance coaching is not cheerleading. It is not building up a salesperson's self-esteem, or tearing it down. Nor should it be a waste of time. It is simply this: *Helping the salesperson adopt behaviors that cause closed sales and remove behaviors that stand in the way of closing sales.* That's it.

The Current Situation

There is a reason why most sales managers don't know how to coach. It is a sad corporate tale that unfolds like this:

Stage one, the promotion: The sales star becomes a sales manager. He does not know the first thing about coaching people. He only knows how to sell. However, upon receiving his promotion he now knows he is tasked with making his salespeople into better performers. Unfortunately, no one above this newbie manager knows how to coach; and the previous people, now long forgotten, didn't know either. The newbie goes out into the field armed with self-confidence and supported by complete corporate ignorance.

Stage two, the coach is coached: The new manager tells his boss he is going to travel with an under-performing salesperson and is told: "Your job is to make this kid better. Clone yourself. Make him into a 'you.' Watch him. Give him feedback." This is now the sum total of training the newbie manager receives on the art of sales performance coaching.

Stage three, the coach starts coaching: The newbie manager travels with a struggling salesperson and gives this underperformer feedback, "You probably know your numbers are awful and they need to improve. When I was selling, I'd do it this way. My numbers were always good so this should improve your numbers too." Unfortunately, the newbie manager really doesn't have a clear picture of what it was that made him successful, because he could not step outside of his body and watch himself selling, so he shares an unclear picture of what the struggling salesperson should do. The salesperson thinks, "What a jerk. Typical newbie boss. Tells me to do a whole lot of nothing."

Stage four, the coach stops coaching: The newbie boss can see that this giving-advice garbage doesn't work, but knows he is tasked with improving their performance. On each successive sales trip he elbows the salesperson out of the way and begins to take over the sales call. "If they can't close a sale, then I will," he tells himself, and adds, "How else will I get their numbers up?" Unfortunately, now he will never know what his salespeople are doing well, because he doesn't give them a chance to sell. And he can't see what they are doing wrong, because they don't get a chance to show those behaviors either.

Stage five, lather, rinse, repeat: After a few years of futility these underachievers receive a new boss who receives the same training in coaching and soon rediscovers the joy of selling.

First-line sales managers are one of the most under-utilized assets in corporate America. Effective behaviors close sales, and sales managers can equip salespeople with these behaviors through coaching. There is no other position that can have such a dramatic impact on the performance of salespeople and the growth of sales revenue. But for this asset to be utilized, sales managers have to know how to coach. This chapter will attempt to impart this skill to those sales managers who have the drive to continually improve.

What Coaching Can Look Like

We've already been through one coaching session in this book and it was hugely successful. It was one of the toughest sales challenges a sales performance coach can face: How do I make one of my best salespeople/sales managers better? What makes this a tough challenge is the enormous ego that successful salespeople often have. This ego can serve a salesperson well when they need to deal with rejection, but it can also stand in the way of their learning from others.

Do you remember the story of the senior salesperson who presented product in a dated manner, using too much text, and black and white photos on his slides? That was an example of the first step in sales performance coaching; we observe which success behaviors are missing and which bad behaviors need to be removed. The second stage is selling the salesperson on the need to adopt the new behavior.

We witnessed stage two when I performed a live demonstration for the salesperson in front of an important group of customers. He then followed and was able to compare their reactions to both presentations. His behavior changed after he saw the value of the new approach. A good salesperson became better after adopting successful sales presentation behaviors.

Finding the Success Behaviors

You will likely know some of the sales behaviors associated with success, but it is doubtful you will know all of them. A way to find out more of these behaviors, and then impart them to your team, is to do the following. Travel with a salesperson who is in the middle of the pack. Observe how he sells as closely as you can. Note some of his behaviors that you thought were successful and others that needed changing. Then go travel with your very best.[23]

When you work with your best salesperson you have this goal: To discover what sales behaviors he expresses that the average performer does not. Once you discover what behaviors your star utilizes that the rest of your representatives do not, you possess a powerful tool to improve your sales team's performance, and one that does not take much selling to get them to adopt. Most salespeople look up to the salesperson who is always finishing first. Therefore, when you coach your salespeople on this behavior you need simply ask, "If I was to tell you what Bill does that makes a huge difference in his selling, would you be interested in finding that out?"

The Limits of Coaching

It is virtually certain they will want to know what Bill, the sales star, is doing to be so successful. But here is where coaching can hit a wall. You may have a salesperson who has an un-teachable spirit.

---

[23] Neil Rackham and Richard Ruff, *Managing Major Sales* (New York: Harper Collins, 1991). The reason why you don't travel with the worst and the best salespeople is because the worst may lack every successful behavior, while the average salespeople may be missing just one or two key behaviors. These ideas, and others in this chapter on sales performance coaching, come from this footnoted reference. Since reading *Managing Major Sales* early in my career, I have tested their coaching ideas extensively and find they work exceptionally well. If you are a sales manager you will benefit from reading this excellent work.

Typically, these people are middle-of-the-pack performers possessed by an arrogant regard for their abilities that is completely out of touch with reality. In their prideful spirit they tend to look down on most everyone, particularly coaches, because by diminishing everyone else they feel they are elevated to their rightful mountaintop. If a salesperson has an un-teachable spirit, then they cannot be coached and need to be replaced.

Another expression of the un-teachable spirit is the person who is comfortable being mediocre. For a person to be successful they must be *able* to do what their job requires, and have the *desire* to do it. For example, let's say I want to be a quantum physicist. This desire is not enough for me to succeed. I also need, among other things, advanced mathematical skills—the ability—and these I do not possess. Desire without abilities leads to failure, as does abilities without desire. You need both to succeed.

You can coach many people to develop sales abilities, but you cannot give the unmotivated person a heart that burns to succeed. They either have it or they don't. Those who do not care to put forth the effort to be successful also have no business in sales.

Another limitation is the way some sales calls are not suitable venues for coaching. For example, when you are making an important presentation for a large piece of business, then everyone involved in the sales call should have a role in making it a success. If the salesperson is struggling to answer a question, and you can help the cause, then do so. But if the call is not of this nature, then it will serve well for coaching.

Coaches During the Sales Call

Coaches are observers of behavior. They want to see what behaviors a salesperson employs when selling. They do not sell. For when a coach starts selling they interfere with the salesperson's behaviors. The sales manager may then coach this salesperson to do exactly what they were just about to do. Then, when the salesperson angrily responds, "I was just about to do that, but you butted in on the sales call!" how will you know if they are telling the truth or not? You won't, so you have to take their word for it and move on. However,

Sales Performance Coaching

when you are quiet there is nowhere for the salesperson who needs coaching to hide, and the good salespeople don't want to hide, because they want to get better at what they do.

Coaches must develop a coaching mindset. Turn coaching into an interesting game of detection, and be motivated by the blessings good coaching can confer: When you coach someone in sales and lift their performance level up from mediocrity to excellence, then you have changed their life for the better. From now on they will enjoy their job more, because they are not only better at it, they are good at it.

Sales management can be a real pain, but making a difference in someone's life is something that will stay with you a lot longer than the buzz you may get from a closed sale. So, embrace coaching if you are a sales manager. If you are a salesperson embrace being coached, because the mindset of a champion seeks constructive criticism. He wants to know what successful sales behaviors he can add to increase his close rate.

The Three Phases of Selling

There are three phases to selling and they are: Preparation, execution and follow-up. All three of these phases have important behaviors associated with success, but we tend to focus on the execution phase, namely, the sales presentation. In this section, I will focus on the all-important preparation phase.

Some of the most important behaviors associated with sales success are found in the preparation phase:

- Developing questions.
- Asking these questions, along with follow-up questions, and taking good notes.
- Developing stories around their important emotional triggers.
- Developing a differentiation presentation that advantageously compares your product to your competitor's.

- Developing a script for each slide.
- Developing memorable phrases.
- Developing a TV-like presentation.
- Rehearsing until the presentation is mastered.

As a coach, you will want to check on these behaviors before the presentation, or else, when the big money decision is on the line, you may come up quite short. Some of the specific things you can check before the presentation are:

Question Quality

If they've conducted the needs analysis already, then what questions did they use? What answers did they get? Did they ask effective follow-up questions? Were the questions tailored to the different decision influencers and the decision makers?

A tailored question to an IT professional might be, "How high of a priority is it for you to maximize company productivity through your network?" This can be followed by an open-ended question, "What other goals do you have?" "Are you trying to get rid of other problems that we haven't talked about?"

Analyzing the Analysis

Did he uncover any information that gives him an edge? Were there any items that seemed particularly important? How does he plan on using this information? Did he record the exact words of the decision maker in order to use them during his presentation?

If the entire exercise generated little of value, then where did the salesperson go wrong? Were the questions wrong? Did he treat his customer interview as just another meaningless exercise required by management?

Presentation Development

There are many important areas in a presentation that the coach should look for. Prior to the presentation check on some of the following areas:

1. Style: Is the look and feel of the presentation cluttered, text-centric, devoid of images, graphs, embedded videos, and so on. If so, this needs to be changed.

2. Are there interesting, memorable stories inserted into the presentation at appropriate intervals?

3. Is there repetition with variation of the emotionally important solutions targeting the decision maker and the influencers?

4. If your salesperson is presenting with another person, have they rehearsed together?

Relationships

Does he have strong relationships at this account? Are they with the decision maker and the influencers? How deep do they go? Does he know details about their personal lives? What are their avocations? Does he have a plan to develop relationships throughout his territory and, specifically, for this account?

Territory Management

Is his funnel filled with new opportunities? Are they being advanced, meaning: Do they all have a next step and a date? If the funnel isn't full, then has he mapped out where the older, replaceable systems in his market are? Has he visited them to see if they are considering replacing their old system?

Many preparation behaviors cause sales success. Several of these contribute to a successful presentation, while others are not concerned with the presentation at all. If these behaviors are missing, then they need to be added to your salesperson's repertoire. If they are present but poorly executed, then the salesperson needs coaching to improve their impact.

Just as there can be bad selling, there can also be harmful sales performance coaching. The following guidelines and tips, if followed, should limit the destruction and improve the instruction.

Coaching Tips and Guidelines

Salespeople who are being coached are emotionally exposed and vulnerable. Therefore, if you are to have a hope of positively changing their behavior, then you need to earn their trust every coaching hour of the day. This is accomplished by following these guidelines.

Be Gentle

Personalities need to be taken into account when delivering a coaching critique. I've worked with star performers who were great at selling and were even better when it came to beating themselves up. Some of your best performers will have an obsessive-compulsive component to their personality that will make them obsess over the smallest criticism for days. Literally. Therefore, it is always wise to be gentle in the delivery of any critique, and for those who routinely beat themselves up a critique is not even necessary. Simply show them what you've seen others do, let them know how well it has worked for them, and how the next time you work together you'd like to see them doing it too. Then end this by sincerely praising the things they are doing well.

Some may think, "Hey, they're just going to have to get over it. I'm not going to walk on egg shells just because they're weird." Okay. But when this high performer stops performing, or finds another job, then who loses? Besides, their obsessive-compulsive nature might be what makes them so good at what they do. So why treat someone poorly because of the way they are wired when this wiring is what makes them so successful?

Praise

It is especially important for a coach to praise the person he is coaching; otherwise, the person being coached will begin to think his boss can only see the negative things he is doing. We used the following rule during our training-class critiquing sessions: Before anything could be said about areas of potential improvement, the salesperson needed to be praised for all of the right things they were doing. It let them know that we didn't just see bad things during their presentation.

Every coaching session should begin with praise that is accurate and believable. False flattery does little to build up the credibility of a coach. The praise also needs to be valued. "Hey, I really like the way you organize your trunk," may be accurate, but who cares. How I organize my trunk has no impact on my sales success. I can have a trunk that looks like it belongs to a hoarder and can still be very successful in sales.

Therefore, praise them on things they are doing well that are directly tied to their sales success. For example, "You really listen well. You never interrupt your customer; and you have a great ability to get them to talk about important things that will help you close sales."

Put praiseworthy behaviors in a follow-up letter to the salesperson and in their annual review. This is especially true of behaviors that they have learned from your coaching and have demonstrated in the field.

If they are truly exceptional in an area you've observed, then get the CEO of the company, or the highest-ranking person available to you, to send him an email saying, "I've heard great things about your work in the field." Words can generate positive emotions that will help a salesperson find a gear they never knew they had as they move toward higher heights.

I am always amazed at how simple and easy praising someone is, how profound its impact can be, and how so few people seem to connect these dots and praise their employees. Words of praise have emotional power. They cost nothing to use and, depending upon who says them, can be treasured by those who receive them.

Rewarding Good Behavior

Good behaviors and outcomes should be praised *and rewarded*, and the cost can be insignificant in comparison to its impact. A sales manager should have a small budget that gives him the ability to reward salespeople at his discretion. If he has ten salespeople, then this budget could be as low as $2,500 each year. Then, when someone closes a big sale, or does anything that is both important and exceptional, they can be given a $250 gift card redeemable at their favorite clothing store, restaurant, spa, whatever, but it can't be money. And if that is too rich, then make it a $100 gift card. The purpose is to create a good memory, and to say thanks for a job well done. If money goes unspent, then some of it can go into the next year's pot.

Sometimes the unexpected kindness is the one that has the most impact. The dollar amount is not critical. It is the simple fact that excellence often goes unrecognized, or uncommented upon, and this program attempts to reverse that regrettable trend. It also attempts to create a culture wherein management is on the lookout for opportunities to praise and reward their salespeople.

Focus

Every salesperson will have areas they can improve on, and in most cases the list of possible improvements is long. However, your goal is to change their behavior and this means your list for them will always be short. You will focus on one behavior for them to work on, two at most—e.g., a good behavior to add and a bad behavior to get rid of.

This may seem like we are setting the bar too low, but we aren't. We are simply trying to create a process that delivers the result we seek: behavior change. Since it is difficult to change one behavior, why make it exponentially more difficult by having a coaching candidate try to change three or four behaviors at the same time? Besides, as you will see in the story at the end of this chapter, getting them to adopt just one behavior is often enough to take them from failure to success.

One's focus also needs to be limited to working with only one or two coaching candidates at a time. This is because coaching candidates require a significant time investment, and managers have only so much time to give.

Since coaches need to limit their efforts to one or two behaviors, the coach must prioritize which behavior is the most important. Then this behavior will be the focus of the coaching sessions that follow.

Sales Performance Coaching

Selling the Program

Most salespeople have an innate desire to do well. The more competitive ones desire to be the best. They also realize sales managers are supposed to offer suggestions about how they can improve. But a coaching program is not about tips or suggestions. It is about a coach working with a salesperson who understands that the addition or subtraction of a single behavior can make a good salesperson great, and a great salesperson even better.

If a sales team resists coaching, then the following points need to be made to help get them on board:

1. No one can see himself selling. Therefore, a salesperson may not realize they are doing something that impedes their success.

2. You will be observing what the best performers are doing, and will be helping others adopt these winning actions.

3. This coaching exercise is cooperative and will be marked by open discussion.

4. Improvements will be reflected in annual reviews and annual reviews impact compensation.

The benefit of coaching is judged in one way, and only one way. Does it lead to sales revenue growth? If it does, then coaching is an obvious benefit to the salesperson whose compensation should increase as he grows the company's revenue.

Summary of Some Important Points

Success in coaching comes from acting according to several clear and specific guidelines:

1. The sales presentation is not the only focus of coaching. The preparation and follow-up behaviors are also important.

2. The coach is totally focused on the salesperson's behaviors.

3. The goal is not to deliver a comprehensive critique, but to change behavior.

4. Because behavior change is difficult, a coach should focus on one behavior at a time.

From the Bottom to the Top

Joe was a Region Manager whose toes were curling over the edge of the sales abyss, the pit where ineffective salespeople are consigned. He was nearing retirement, posting horrendous numbers, losing important accounts and, to make matters worse, customers were calling me to tell me he was no longer allowed in their hospital.

What was I to do? The reflexive response these days is, "Fire the bum!" But he wasn't a bum, so I decided I would try and transform Joe's sales performance through coaching. However, I must make an admission that discredits me: I wasn't hopeful. I believed he was probably set in his ways, and this coaching exercise would be a case of simply going through the motions.

Removing Negative Behaviors

The first thing I had to figure out was something that utterly mystified me. Joe was liked by everyone in our organization, and just about everyone he met, so how could he be angering nursing staffs to the point where they called corporate to bar him from their account? The first time he was barred I believed it was an anomaly. The second time it occurred, not long after the first occurrence, I saw a trend emerging and became concerned.

I was traveling with Joe to discover how he was upsetting customers, and on one occasion a customer asked if our product could do something it couldn't do. Joe answered, "I don't think that would be a really good idea. Do you?" They worked it out in a brief back and forth, and I let it pass. There was a little bit of a demeaning tone to his response, but it was a one-time event, and my mindset about Joe was that he was uniformly nice.

The next day of our travel a nurse brought up an objection during his presentation and he responded, "I don't see how that could be a problem." I rushed in, "What he means is, it is not a problem for many of our customers, but here are some things we could do to make sure it is not a problem for you."

The look the customer gave Joe, while she thanked me, was one of anger and disdain. I now knew what behaviors Joe was engaging in that got him kicked out of two hospitals. He was responding to a customer's questions and objections in a demeaning, belittling fashion that seemed to suggest their questions were somehow stupid. Worse yet, he seemed to be completely unaware of the impact it was having.

After we finished, I asked Joe if he knew why he was kicked out of two accounts recently. He said he didn't. I told him I thought I knew because of what I'd seen during his presentations, and shared with him what he was saying and how the customer responded to it. I then modeled for him a few ways to respond to customer objections, and he noted them.

Old or not, Joe was more than capable of changing his behavior. He must have stopped responding to his customers in a way that angered them, because I never got a call again or saw him behave in that way.

Adding Positive Behaviors

The next step in my coaching was to teach Joe how to differentiate. I went over it a couple of times, gave him some of the slides to present, and asked him if he felt like he would be ready for the presentation tomorrow afternoon. He said he believed he was ready. I had my doubts, so I offered to share the load and make half of the presentation, but he said he would be fine.

Joe got up to present and if he was nervous I couldn't tell. I was nervous for him, but I tried not to show it. He started by creating the mindset of how he was an honest broker of objective information, and then he proceeded to show the customer how our product delivered solutions that our competitors could not. The Chief Nursing Officer had seen enough. She was sold. They started mapping out what needed to be done to get our system installed.

You could have knocked me over with a feather. Joe was masterful. I would not have changed a thing. He was like a minor leaguer who marched up to the plate, faced the best pitcher in baseball, and hit it straight out of the park on his first swing. And the good news is he got better.

Joe's numbers began to climb and he went from the bottom to the top of the heap. I had a team of very strong Region Managers, and Joe was now one of the best. Two years later he won the Region Manager of the Year award.

Conclusion

We underestimate the impact sales performance coaching can have. It can turn a dud into a superstar, and can result in revenue growth that far exceeds what was once thought possible. It also has a positive impact on the coach. Instead of writing pink slips he gets to help a struggling person become a star performer who is treated by his peers with the respect reserved for the truly talented.

Many Region Managers can feel like they are babysitters. They check expense reports for accuracy. They travel with their salespeople to see if they are familiar with their territory, or their customers. They check to see if they know the basics and can sell. But until a sales manager is able to make salespeople substantially better than they once were, the sales manager will remain an asset that is failing to return its full value. Learning how to coach a salesperson can change this.[24]

We are now going to the final section of this book. It is one that takes advantage of the lessons we have learned and applies them to an area where everyone eventually gets a chance to test their selling skills: the world of interviewing.

---

[24] For those organizations interested in making all of their first-line sales managers more productive, please send a note to tom@essentialgrowthsolutions.com.

Part Four:

Everyone Sells

14: Interviewing

The interview is perhaps the most pressure-packed sales situation there is, and it requires selling one of the most awkward and difficult of "products"—oneself. Worse yet, most people who are interviewing for a job don't know how to sell. They are like people who have never driven a car before, are shown the brake and the gas pedal, and are then set loose on Germany's autobahn.

The results? Interviewees typically use a strategy that is the exact opposite of the one they should be using. I've seen this in every interviewing seminar I've conducted over the last ten years. And I made the same mistakes until I learned the skills detailed in this chapter. Then, after I learned them, I became the far-less-qualified candidate who was able to get the job.

The following is a true story:

> At one point in my career I had held four jobs during the previous five years. Twice I chose to leave for a better opportunity, once a toxic culture disgorged me and I was the last hired before a bankruptcy reorganization. My resume was a disaster. Then I found out about a great opportunity. It was a National Sales Director position that would involve hiring a national sales team, training them, and launching a revolutionary new monitor used during childbirth.
>
> I had no experience in obstetrics and I was competing against someone who had twenty years of experience with the

world's number one medical monitoring company. He came personally recommended by the doctor who authored a textbook on obstetrics used by medical students.

It gets worse. This professor/MD/author worked for the hiring company as a consultant. Nonetheless, I got the job.

Our starting point is the one area most interviewing courses fail to address: understanding the sales process as it relates to the interview.

The Complex Sales Process and the Interview

"What causes the hiring decision?" Once we correctly answer this question, we possess a key that can guide our actions to cause this hiring-decision-effect.

Previously we've noted how complex sales are closed, or caused, by emotions. Complex sales typically involve:

1. A decision maker and several decision influencers.

2. Spending a relatively large sum of money.

3. The results of a bad decision can haunt the decision maker for years.

Now compare that to the hiring decision. It typically involves:

1. A decision maker and several decision influencers.

2. Spending a relatively large sum of money.

3. The results of a bad decision can haunt the decision maker for years.

I apologize for being so repetitive.

In complex sales there are often several presentations. In interviewing there are often several interviews with the decision maker and decision influencers. Both the decision to buy an expensive product and the decision to hire an interviewing candidate have risks. For example, the high cost of a bad hiring decision includes: the money and time wasted on training, the money and time now needed to find another new hire, damage to the reputation

Interviewing

of the one who showed such poor judgment in making the hire, and the list goes on.

Therefore, the hiring decision is affected by emotions like fear. It is also affected by the emotion of hope, the possibility of hiring a star. In other words, like the complex sales decision, the hiring decision is caused by emotions. These two decision-making processes are virtually identical. This is why this entire book on selling can help the interviewing candidate, because the techniques used in complex sales are virtually the same as those used to "sell" the interviewee to an interviewer.

The Typical Mindset of the Interviewee

Some of the emotional drivers of the interviewer's decision are: Do they like you? Do you make them feel uncomfortable or comfortable? Do they trust you? However, most people act as if the hiring decision is the outcome of a rational thought process. So, they attempt to sell themselves by engaging in a mind-numbing data dump. They think they will be hired if they give the most reasons why they would be perfect for the job. Since they only have an hour to make their points—all 100 of them—they dump at a furious pace.

This is a losing strategy. The opposite approach is required. Emotionally caused decisions are not arrived at by way of data, statistics, reasons and rationality. Your interviewer may have four or more candidates to sort through before the interviewees go to the next round. If you were sitting for hours on end, and had candidate after candidate pummel you with facts at a rate your mind could not possibly absorb, how would you respond?

Your brain, out of self-defense, would tune out this noise. The same thing happens when a jackhammer working on a street outside your home or office is making its racket. You tune it out. The interviewer, who is being barked at by candidates, responds in like manner to this noise. And when the interview ends, and the candidate leaves after receiving assurances that he made a great impression, the interviewer prints on the top of the resume, "Not in a million years."

Just as in sales, the war we must win in an interview is the one within. We are faced with fears about our future and, like a drowning person, we flail and fight the one who can keep us from sinking. In our insecurity we try to impress the interviewer with how great we are, and never stop to think, "How well does this approach work in the real world?"

You've probably met a person at a party who drops names, talks up their accomplishments, etc., all within the first few moments of meeting him. What was your impression? Did you not want to run in the opposite direction? So why would this impression change just because we've entered a situation called an interview?

"Wait!" you might respond, "I was told by all of the interviewing authorities that you've got to sell yourself during an interview." True, but if you've read the previous pages, then you know how people hate to be sold, but enjoy buying. Therefore, you will need to use those same techniques, detailed in the previous chapters, to cause the buying/hiring decision.

I will not cover every technique used in the preceding pages because it would take too much time to do so, but I will cover a few of the ones that have the greatest impact on an interview. Then, if you are interested in learning the entire interviewing system, you can go to www.nomedalforsecondplace.com to read a sample chapter from my book on interviewing.

One of the most powerful techniques is one we've covered already in some detail. It enables you to sell yourself in a way that doesn't feel like a sales pitch.

Storytelling Magic

I wrote about how I was faced with an almost impossible job opportunity at the beginning of this chapter. After I landed the job I had to ask the interviewer why I was hired over the much more qualified person. The answer, "You had such great stories." I'm not making this up.

I took the time to create about ten stories that highlighted specific achievements, and they gave me a tremendous advantage. While my competitor for the job was likely relating dry facts and figures about his strong accomplishments, I was communicating mine to the

Interviewing

interviewer's heart and soul. Stories are memorable, entertaining and they can be moving. They also take hours of work to develop and refine. Because of this, few people will take the time to craft them, but if you do... advantage: yours.

After writing and rewriting them several times, stories are easy to memorize. What I would do is rehearse saying them from memory while being timed and taped. I wanted to see how long they took and how my voice sounded. Was I talking too fast? Did my voice convey warmth, energy and enthusiasm?

There was another benefit gained from this preparation. After going through this process my confidence increased, because I now knew I was capable of delivering an award-winning performance. Confidence and competence emanate from a person who has taken the time to master the interviewing process, and the impression this makes can generate the emotion of trust.

Your first step is to look at the things you have done and make a list of some of your most important achievements. Let's say you are in manufacturing and you were able to reduce manufacturing's error-rate from one error per 1,000 opportunities to one error per 500,000 opportunities.

When the interviewer asks you a question like, "What achievement are you proudest of?" One way to answer this question is, "I'm proudest of reducing the error rate at my current company by five hundredfold." But is this a memorable way of framing your proudest achievement? Hardly. It is a dry, forgettable data point. Instead, answer as follows:

> What am I proudest of? When I joined Acme the company had a reputation for putting out the lowest-quality product in our industry, and the manufacturing team had high turnover and very low morale.
>
> To turn this situation around I developed a plan with measurable milestones and whenever we achieved one we would have a mini-celebration. We focused on process improvements and began to build quality into the product.

Before you knew it, we became a team and the quality gains we produced were dramatic. We reduced the failure rate five hundredfold. Instead of one error per 1,000 opportunities it became one per 500,000. This reduced the cost of manufactured goods by 10%. Margins improved for the first time in five years. The estimated annual impact was $200,000 to the bottom line. And our internal surveys showed my manufacturing team went from being among the least satisfied employees to the most satisfied in the company.

Now imagine you are the one who is conducting the interview. Which answer—the dry data-point or the story—would prove to be the most interesting and memorable? Which one depicted the actual impact of the numeric improvement in the failure-rate reduction?

When interviewing, you may be up against people who have far more impressive achievements than you; but if your achievements are fully fleshed out through the medium of stories, then they appear to be more significant than your competitor's. For example, a competitor might say, "I am proudest of the fact that I reduced the error rate from one every 1,000 opportunities, to one every 1,000,000." Rationally speaking, this statistic is twice as good as the achievement detailed in the above story, but somehow it seems less powerful than the story of a transformational manager who turned his demoralized team around.

Embedded Stories

People begin to remember things that are repeated with variation, and part of the interview's challenge is to be remembered, to separate oneself from the pack. We can repeat the above story with variation by embedding it in our resume. It can appear in some of the resume's bullet points:

- **Leadership:** Turned a demoralized team with high turnover into a highly motivated group with lowest turnover rate in company.

- **Quality:** Turned lowest quality product in industry into its highest, by reducing defect rate five hundredfold.

Interviewing

The interviews are over and the interviewer looks through the stack of resumes and sees the above bullet points. They trigger the memory of your story and she thinks, "Oh yeah, I remember that. What a great story. He inherited a demoralized group doing shoddy work and turned them into a group celebrating their newfound success."

"Oh, come on," some may protest, "no one will remember your stories." To this I offer my experience. Why was I hired over a much more qualified individual? My new boss answered, "You had such great stories." In other words, they were not just remembered, they were the difference.

After remembering one of your stories, does the interviewer then say, "He's the one. Let's extend him an offer." Maybe, but one story, or one skill set, does not a sale make in most cases. Therefore, our goal is to accumulate advantages that enable us to separate ourselves from the crowd. We are trying to distance ourselves from the blur that accompanies the complex sales process. We want to be the high-definition image while our competitors are lost somewhere on a snowy screen.

Calling Bitter, Party of One!

Jack had no problem getting an interview. Everyone who looked at his resume of achievements wanted him on their team…until they met him. During interviews they would discover he had a tape replaying in his head about how he was treated so unfairly by his last boss. It was so unjust! He had a right to be angry! The interview would end and the tape in his head rewound until it returned to its root of bitterness. He loved his bitterness, snuggled up next to it, and refused to let it go.

Do you know why 'Bitter' is always a party of one? It's because no one wants to be around a bitter person.

I got a chance to meet Jack at an employment workshop I was conducting pro-bono at my church. I was going over how you need to be universally positive during your interview, because positive emotions tend to generate positive emotions, while negative ones generate the bad vibes that result in someone else winning the job.

The Causes of Sales Success

I then said:

> I don't care if you're last boss was unjust, unfair, a nasty tyrant who should never manage another soul. If you've had a boss like this, and the interviewer asks you, "How would you describe your last boss?" You respond, "He was a great teacher. I learned more from him than possibly any other boss I've worked for." And you say this because he did teach you not to do the things he did. Remember to never be negative.

Jack exploded, "I couldn't say that. I couldn't say anything positive about a man who lied compulsively and treated me the way he did."

I asked Jack, "Have you ever expressed this bitterness during an interview?"

He thought about it and said, "Yes, I suppose I have."

I asked, "Since your bad experience with your former boss, have you ever made it to the second round of interviews?"

He answered, "No."

I then explained how bitterness was an interview killer, and how no interviewer cared about his bitterness and anger, except in this way: It's not their problem and they want to keep it that way. "So they don't hire you," I said, and then asked, "Now would you choose someone who was bitter and angry over someone who was charming and positive?"

Jack wasn't about to let go of his bitterness without a fight. He said, "I would choose the person with the best skills."

Like many people, he thought his credentials and achievements would cause the hiring decision. So I said, "But you know the most qualified person does not always get the job offer. I bet you were more accomplished than every candidate who was hired instead of you.

"So why do interviewers bypass better-qualified candidates? It is because the hiring decision is emotional, not rational, and bitterness is emotionally repulsive. Until you get over your bitterness, no one will hire you."

Interviewing

He still resisted accepting responsibility for his interviewing failures. His false assumptions, mindsets and arrogance kept him from seeing what seemed so obvious to me, so I said to the workshop attendees, "We are not here to gang up on Jack; we are here to help him. It could be I am misreading him entirely. Does anyone else feel he is expressing his bitterness in a way that might prevent his being hired?"

They supported my view, and our consensus opened Jack's eyes. I concluded with this advice, "Try to do only one thing in your next interview. Emanate warmth and see what happens."

Days later he was interviewed for the umpteenth time and was hired.

Jack was not a pleasant person. He came across as surly, self-righteous, brooding and unhappy. In his case his behaviors—what we could see and hear—probably matched his thoughts and feelings. But in the case of many interviewees, their inside is not matched by their outside. Like Jack, they fail to smile during interviews and seem too intense. Some of their answers can have a negative edge to them.

We need to commit to being only positive and never negative during an interview. This is because human beings are like emotional tuning forks. They assume the tone of the tuning fork they are near. In other words, when we are near a sad person, we can become sad. When we are near an intense person, we start to feel like we just drank a triple expresso. Therefore, we need to always be positive if we are to cause a positive outcome.

The war we must win is the one fought within. We cannot allow our negative feelings to spill over into the interviewing arena. Few things are as harmful to your chance of success as this.

Everyone Has Weak Spots

The first rule about weak spots is stop talking so much. When a person takes the stand and the prosecuting attorney asks him, "Did you steal this computer we found in your possession?" The accused does not answer, "Of course. But there's more. I stole five laptops from a computer store. You haven't solved that crime yet, have you?

And wait, don't interrupt me with another question, because there is so much more to tell…"

The point is, when a question is asked about an area where you have a weakness do not volunteer more information than you absolutely have to. The goal is to emulate the iceberg. Most of an iceberg's mass is under the surface of the water. When it comes to that which is hurtful to your job search you keep as much of it beneath the surface as possible. This is not lying; it is simply refusing to commit suicide during an interview.

For example, if they ever ask you, "Were you terminated from your last job?" and you were terminated after your company was bought out, the answer is not, "Yes, I was terminated." It is, "I was downsized after our company was purchased."

You are merely casting what occurred in your past in the most favorable light with the most favorable terms. Again, you are not required to do the bidding of the prosecuting attorney when they are attempting to convict you. The same is true when the interviewer is wearing his prosecuting-attorney cap.

Let's replay the question, "Were you terminated?" You answer, "Yes." This leads to, "Why were you terminated?" Does this line of questioning look like it will turn out well for you?

The iceberg technique is designed to limit an interviewer's gleeful pursuit of hurtful information. The good news is this sort of inquisition rarely happens to the person who has developed a positive emotional connection with the interviewer through non-verbal behaviors (smiles, handshake, tone, posture, etc.), stories, memorable phrases, and so on. The interviewer not only expects this type of candidate to do well in the interview, he also wants him to do well.

Closing

Websites by the hundred will tell you, "Asking for the job is the most important thing most interviewees forget to do." Please don't listen to that silliness. The interview is a complex sale. It is not ruled by the "close, close, close" mentality of simple sales. However, you do ask to be part of the ongoing process. For example, instead of asking, "When do I start?"—the assumptive close—you restate how you meet their criteria, and then ask a question that shows you respect their process and want to continue to be a part of it:

> You mentioned the three highest qualifications you had were X, Y, and Z. I believe I've showed how I meet these criteria by the way I've proven I've done X, have achieved Y, and Z characterizes my entire career. So my last question is this: is there anything that you've heard or seen that prevents me from going to the next step of this process?

If they answer, "No. You seem to be a good fit. Of course we'll need to get back and talk amongst ourselves before we can decide on the final slate of candidates."

You reply, "I understand. So, in anticipation of me making that final slate, what will be the next step of the process? Has that been determined?"

And with that information you thank your last interviewer, leave and immediately find a quiet place to write down everything you've observed. What questions did they ask? This will show what they are trying to uncover, and are interested in either getting or avoiding. What are the social styles of the interviewers? Were there red flags? This could be a bad situation that you are better off avoiding. What answers of mine seemed to resonate with the interviewers? Was there a question that I fumbled? How can I answer it better?

Then call the company's switchboard, ask to be put into the various interviewers' voicemail boxes and leave brief, professional voicemails thanking them for their time. Tell them you hope to join a great team that works for a respected company. This is followed by an email and snail mail. The snail mail can be a nice touch, particularly when it is on nice stationery. The purpose of this is to show the interviewer the strength of your follow-up skills.

Conclusion

These techniques work along with the others detailed in *No Medal for Second Place: How to Finish First in Job Interviews*. If you diligently apply them, then you will likely have a leg up on your competition. They may be more qualified than you, but what speaks louder, statistics on a page or a more impressive candidate in the flesh?

By mastering this situation, known as the interview, you will generate feelings of trust, "This candidate seems to really be on top of things." Interviews can be intimidating and stressful, but if you make it seem like a walk in the park, because you are so well prepared, then the interviewer will think, "At least one candidate seems to be up to this challenge."

This leads me to my final word of advice for both job seekers and salespeople who are trying to close the biggest sale of their life: *prepare*.

Those who work hard during the preparation phase, on developing the perfect solution for the buying or hiring decision makers, are armed with powerful advantages. The results can be astonishing. This is not magic, but it sometimes seems like it.

15: Fulfillment

The Engineering Project

An engineer had an idea about how to make his company's product better. He had heard enough of the complaints from sales and marketing about how the user interface was clunky, not intuitive in the least, and a major reason why they were losing market share.

After spending days of thinking about what their product was supposed to do for customers, he came up with a simpler design. He ruthlessly cut away everything but the essentials. He developed cost estimates and development timelines and presented it to his boss who promptly told him he hated it, and if he ever saw a copy of this idea floating around the office he would be fired.

He left his boss's office feeling confused, angry and demoralized. He knew the idea he presented was excellent. It accomplished what customers said they wanted. It was elegant. The costs were acceptable. The payback would probably be measured in months. So, what went wrong?

He failed to see how his great idea might be perceived as threatening to a boss who felt very insecure in his position. He also failed to notice how his boss had a slightly paranoid streak that generated the conviction that all of his subordinates were after his job—and some were. His proposal generated feelings of fear, and emotions like fear cause irrational decisions like the one his boss made.

What is more, he never considered in his entire working life how he would have to sell an idea, even a good idea, if it were ever to be implemented. He never thought he might need to learn how to sell to fulfill his dreams and ambitions.

Engineering, Accounting, etc., and Sales

If you work outside of the field of sales, it is likely you will have a tough time adapting the ideas in this book. However, it is entirely up to you. All that is needed is a mind open to new ideas and a willingness to wrestle with them until they are mastered.

I mention this because I've observed firsthand how difficult it is for other departments to master the sales and marketing process. For example, I've worked with many engineers who were good at what they did, and they believed their intellectual gifts enabled them to be smarter at sales and marketing than those who worked in this department. I know they felt this, because they kept offering advice as to how we could do our job better. The only thing remarkable about their suggestions was the way they were so laughable, botched and lame. I wish I was exaggerating, but I'm not.

Why couldn't they see what was so painfully obvious to us? What probably blinded them was the way their profession shaped their thinking. Their world was rational, math-driven, and rules-based. They were conditioned to think and approach problems in a way that was completely different from the one that should govern the sales process. Sales, as we have seen, must deal with people and the entire messy world of emotions. When it comes to humans there are no linear equations, because the linear world has no foothold in the turbulent, chaotic realm of human emotion.

Yet, no matter what the bias of one's thinking, minds can be opened to new ideas, and they can be utilized. It may take more effort for those conditioned to think in a mathematical, linear way, but it can be done. For example, in my former company many of the sales and marketing people started their careers in engineering.

If the question is, "Why waste my time investing so much energy in learning this skill? I am not going to sell." Then I must inform those who think this way that everyone must sell. Furthermore, if you are unable to sell it can limit the progress you make in your career and the fulfillment you experience in this life.

We return to the engineer who was threatened with being fired if he shared his remarkable idea with anyone else. After being armed with a little sales knowledge, the outcome was much different.

The Engineer Revisited

The engineer who read this book understood he needed to change his boss's perception of him. Since his boss was very insecure about his job, and slightly paranoid about how those beneath him were trying to undermine him, he needed to exhibit behaviors that generated feelings of trust. To navigate the dark maze of human psychology he approached his boss early in his project and said:

> Hey boss, I'm working on our customer interface and I think I've come up with some exciting stuff. But I don't want to work on this alone. I need your help, your feedback, and your ideas. I'd like this to be a joint project, because you will need to be the one who presents it to higher management. I don't think it will take too much of your time, and if it is as good as I think it is, then you'll get huge kudos from higher and I'll get kudos from you. Do you have a minute so I can show it to you?

Instead of perceiving this project as a threat, the boss now sees it as a way of strengthening his reputation with those who he fears might fire him. He also sees his subordinate in a new light. Instead of attempting to subvert him, like he believed every one of his subordinates was trying to do, this subordinate was working to make him look better.

Then, as the project was nearing completion, the engineer again revealed his understanding of the sales process. There were decision makers—the C-level suite—and decision influencers—sales and marketing. If sales and marketing opposed this project, it would likely die. So the engineer went to his boss and said:

> "There's only one way I can see this project failing."

His boss looked shocked and gasped, "How? It's brilliant."

"Sales and marketing might put the kibosh on it just out of pure meanness and spite. So, I have a plan. Let's get them on board before you present it to higher."

"How will you make that happen?"

"We'll show them the project and ask them what they think. They will say, 'I want my team to look it over.' We'll say, 'Cool.' We then show their team the interface. They'll say, 'I want some customers to give me some feedback.' We'll say, 'Cool.' We then show it to their customers. If we have to tweak it some, we do. Then when you go to higher you will have sales and marketing already in your back pocket. The CEO will be even more impressed. What do you think?"

Wow, what a difference possessing the key to the unlit, unforgiving maze of sales can make. Instead of viewing another department as an obstacle to be steamrolled, this approach views them as a customer to be sold, because the goal is not to win a fight, but to cause a favorable decision.

So the engineer who now knows something of the sales process realizes he needs to sell both the decision makers (and this includes his boss), and the influencers, or sales and marketing. He sells sales and marketing by dealing with their emotion of fear.

Those in sales and marketing typically fear engineering-led projects, because they tend to create complex products that satisfy an engineer's inner-geek, but are far less successful with customers. Therefore, the engineer who understands the emotional causes of the "buying" decision eliminates this fear by subjecting his project to some typical sales and marketing processes.

Career Goals Met

What is different between the first story about the creative engineer who fails, and the one about this same person succeeding? Many things, but perhaps the most important difference is this: In the first story the engineer created genuine value, but this real value went

Fulfillment

unrealized and, therefore, remained unreal. In fact, his good work achieved a bad outcome because it damaged his relationship with his insecure, paranoid boss. In the second story, the good produced by the engineer was implemented and all parties benefited—sales and marketing, his boss, the customer and himself. Of these two, who would you prefer to be?

Life can seem unfair because so much of it is subject to irrational forces, like emotions. Until we understand this, accept it, and act according to the peculiarities of human nature, we can be gifted beyond any of our peers and yet live unfulfilled lives. A tree is judged by its fruit, and our lives will likely remain fruitless until we can get others to buy into what we are trying to accomplish.

Emotional Maturity

An unexpected outcome of this "sales" process is the way it requires us to act in an emotionally mature way. It required the engineer to show respect for his boss's emotions even though they were stunted. A wise person understands there is no way we can judge another's emotional development. For if we would have walked an entire life in the moccasins of an emotionally stunted person, and experience what they've experienced, it is likely our emotional development would have been damaged as well.

Wisdom is not required to be an engineer or a salesperson, but this sales system requires acting as if one were wise. It requires respecting a customer's emotions, unless they cross certain lines, because our goal is not to change our customers since we can't, but to sell them since we can.

What is it you seek from your career? Whatever it is, the ability to persuade people will one day help you come closer to realizing your goals. It will enable you to sell your pet projects to others within an organization. And it requires you to act in a way that makes you a better human being. To generate the emotion of trust you will need to be trustworthy. To persuade others you will need to know and respect their feelings. You will do these things because they are the right things to do, and they advance your interests. But more than anything else, you should embrace this path because it can help you live a rewarding life.

Fulfillment

This sales approach can offer significant benefits. It is based on relationships that grow from trust. It can lead to deep friendships that are loving—yes, loving—and ultimately fulfilling in ways that no paycheck, or adrenaline rush from a closed sale, can come close to approximating.

Consultative selling is an attempt to manage the emotional migration of the customer from fear and suspicion to trust and partnership. This migration is one that also needs to be made by the person who endeavors to use this system. While your customers or colleagues learn to trust you, you will learn to trust them, and with every test along the way your relationships can grow and deepen.

Soon you will be calling on friends whose company you have enjoyed for many years, and who will settle for a lesser product so long as you come along with it. You are the one they want to deal with, and you are the one they don't want to lose. As you see your customers battle for you while your company tries to innovate, or even keep up with innovation, as they express genuine caring for your well being, you will begin to realize what you have truly won: their love.

I've known many salespeople who have achieved this. They may not have thought through what the causes of sales success were, but they lived as if they knew them. They developed relationships with their customers to the point of being loved; and they happily returned this love. When they left their territories for another job, or to retire, their customers literally grieved and expressed their sorrow years later. And the salespeople grieved as well, because their business relationship had grown into something more, something fulfilling.

This system of sales is based on the simple notion that emotions are the causes of the buying decision. Its ultimate goal is also emotional. We don't want to merely sell products; we want to live a life that is valued by others. Because in our small sphere—the one we have chosen to work in—we are making a difference by serving our customers, and making their path a little smoother than it would have been without us. This matters to our customers and it should, for these acts of service are no different than the actions that are expected from a trusted friend.

Once you learn how to navigate the maze of human psychology as it relates to buying behavior, you will be able to sell far more effectively. But as with most achievements it requires both working harder and smarter. Focus on adding one successful behavior at a time and your disciplined pursuit of success will be rewarded.

I wish you all the best as you work to master this art of selling, persuading, leading, and causing others to decide in your favor.

www.ingramcontent.com/pod-product-compliance
Lightning Source LLC
Chambersburg PA
CBHW061507180526
45171CB00001B/78